WORKING N
THE SURVIV.

CW00959632

LINDSAY COOK

SIMON & SCHUSTER
A VIACOM COMPANY

The Daily Express parenting site can be found at
www.allaboutparents.com

First published in Great Britain by
Simon & Schuster UK Ltd, 2000
A Viacom Company

1 3 5 7 9 10 8 6 4 2

Simon & Schuster UK Ltd
Africa House
64–78 Kingsway
London WC2B 6AH

Text design: Jane Humphrey
Typeset by: Stylize Digital Artwork
Printed and bound in Italy

A CIP catalogue record for this book is available
from the British Library

ISBN 0 68486 623 4

To Tony
without whom motherhood and this book
would not have been possible,
and also for Rory and Gray
for being great sons and case studies.

CONTENTS:

PREFACE

Superwoman had it easy. All she had to do was save the Universe while wearing a spangly leotard. She did not have to worry about the kids at the same time.

How do you balance a job with bringing up a family? How do you find someone you can trust (and afford) to look after your children? Could you and your partner manage childcare on your own if you both reduced your working hours? How do you tell your boss that you want to work part-time without being demoted? How do you compete against colleagues who have only themselves to look out for?

This book will give you most of the answers. It draws on the experience of dozens of working mothers from contrasting walks of life who have either solved their own problems or can tell the rest of us how to avoid the traps they fell into.

It is aimed at first-time mothers who want to continue to work, especially lone parents. It is also for mothers with older children who want to continue in their jobs or return to work after a break. All need battle plans and a lot of back-up. The following pages will show you how others coped and how their experience can benefit you.

Lindsay Cook

FOREWORD

"Of all the rights of women, the greatest is to be a mother"   Lin Yü-tang

There has always been debate about the role of working mothers in society. The dual responsibility of wage earner and mother is a difficult balancing act. For some working mums there are, quite naturally, feelings of guilt and these often clash with a desire to be independent and to retain financial control. Other parents simply do not have the luxury of choice. Either way, working mums are a fact of life and this emotive issue is set to continue as a significant sociological debate.

Orange is delighted to be associated with this unique guide that lends emotional and practical support to working mums everywhere. Orange has a philosophy based on creating a better world for its customers through simple, accessible, intuitive communication. We are always looking for new ways to help make life easier. The Orange vision was founded on the simple premise that people communicate with people not places, giving increased flexibility for people with busy lives and helping them to communicate wherever, whenever, however they choose.

For mothers everywhere, the future's bright, the future's Orange.

Denise Lewis
Head of Corporate Communications and Sponsorship, Orange

1: YOU ARE NOT ALONE

It is normal for mothers to work. This needs to be said because, not so long ago, it was looked on as abnormal and possibly dangerous. Many in my grandmother's generation were adamant that mothers should stay at home even when their children were at school.

In my home town, the fishing port of Grimsby, such mothers thought it a matter of pride that their children came home from school every day for lunch. It showed they were good and caring mothers. It also made sound economic sense – school dinners were more expensive than home cooking.

Grimsby was a very masculine town. Women were not allowed to work on the fishing boats. They were said to bring bad luck. If they became mothers they were expected to stay at home. They could earn pin money by working a few hours in a shop or doing the ten-till-two shift in the frozen fish factories. But most stayed at home.

This pattern of work was not untypical of many British towns and cities until twenty years ago. Work, much of it in manufacturing industries, was mainly for men. However, in the 1970s and 80s, those industries collapsed and the service sector took over. Suddenly, women were needed as never before. Their skills were often more suited to the new kinds of job. Mothers with young children were welcomed into the workplace, and many were encouraged to have full-time jobs.

The current Government figures are revealing. Almost seven out of ten first-time mothers are back at work within a year. Fifty-three per cent of all mothers with children under five are now out working. We are no longer the exception, we are the rule. Contrast this with the choices faced by mothers before the Second World War. Many lost their jobs when they married. Employers asked probing questions of female interviewees about their marriage plans. If a woman said she might start a family, she would almost certainly fail to get the job.

Today, new laws against sexual discrimination are intended to prevent employers from even asking about a woman's family plans when she arrives for an interview. You can win substantial compensation if you do not get a job for which you are qualified on the grounds that you are pregnant, planning a family or that you have a small child. A teenager from Powys in mid-Wales recently won £4,000 compensation from a supermarket when she was asked if she was pregnant three minutes into an interview for a job as a shelf-stacker. She was eleven weeks pregnant at the time, but the Equal Opportunities Commission told an industrial tribunal that refusing to recruit a woman because she was pregnant was illegal. It was not good enough to assume that a job could not be done by a pregnant woman.

Laws are often broken because employers think they can get away with bad practice. Only a brave few take the bad bosses to court and family-friendly laws take years to be widely observed. For example, it is now theoretically possible for women to win promotion while on maternity leave. But how often does that happen? Why would an employer give someone more responsibilities when she is not at work to carry them out? Only when they read in the newspapers that other firms have had to pay out huge compensation for breaking their promises to women who became pregnant will they change their practice – or become more devious.

Grandmother's generation was far worse off in terms of liberty and equality, but better off in terms of stress. Expectations are now much higher. Most of us want a beautiful, thriving, happy baby, a good relationship with our partner, a stylish home and a fulfilling job. We are under pressure to achieve perfection in all aspects of our lives. But if we set our standards too high in every department, we can end up exhausted and in chaos.

The Australian supermodel Elle Macpherson, nicknamed 'The Body' fell victim to this desire to 'have it all'. She was reputed to be worth £22 million but she did not employ a nanny to help her look after her two-year-old son, Flynn, because she said she wanted to be a full-time mother. However, she collapsed as she was filming for the television comedy *Friends*, exhausted from juggling her work schedule and the care of her child. Married to Swiss banker Arpad Busson, she took her son with her to Los Angeles because she did not want to be parted from him.

Twenty years ago, only a quarter of mothers with babies returned to work before their children were a year old. Now, the vast majority of us are back at work long before the first birthday cake is baked. The reasons are threefold – money, independence and fulfilment.

Most of us, especially lone parents and female breadwinners, need the money. In a survey of a thousand first-time mothers in 1999, 87 per cent said money was their main reason for returning to work, with independence next on the list. With more marriages breaking down, financial independence is seen by women as the best personal insurance. The record of fathers who default on child support means that the choice for mothers whose partners have left the family home is either work or welfare. Poverty damages children, not just while they are young, but well into adult life, as several studies have proved. A job offers a way out of poverty.

We also enjoy work. We like the company and the intellectual stimulation. Women now leave education with equal qualifications to men. We see no reason why we should not have equivalent job satisfaction. In fact, many forward-thinking employers are beginning to see that mothers who work are often more loyal than their male counterparts – as well as being more civilised. We do not like the masculine long-hours culture. But is that a bad thing? Why not work efficiently for eight hours rather than inefficiently for ten?

Working mothers are often more hooked on the idea of stability than their colleagues who do not have children. We do not want to deny ourselves maternity provision by frequent job changes. We like the security blanket of a job where our talents are known and appreciated, rather than the danger of having to strike out and make a name for ourselves all over again. If there are several mothers in a team we are often flexible in helping each other out. Thus it can pay an employer to encourage mothers to stay on.

Motherhood skills can be also be useful at work. It may be hard to believe before you have experienced it, but the tricks used to get a toddler to eat his greens or to clean his teeth can be put to very good use in bringing colleagues into line. I lose count of the times that I have had to remind my workmates that you cannot reward bad behaviour. I did not learn that at business school. I learned it at home with my children.

The tide has turned. Mothers are more valued in the workplace because, quite simply, we are more valuable. We are 'young' twenty years longer than our Victorian or even pre-War counterparts, thanks largely to advances in medical science and contraception. Our biological clocks do not tick as fast. The average age of women having children in Britain is now more than thirty. Many of us leave it until our late thirties or even forties. We can have careers before having children.

In the big cities, this has had a huge impact. At school plays and children's parties in my area of London, I met very few mothers in their twenties. Most had already been working for between fifteen and twenty years. Very few chose to stay at home; they liked going out to work. It would be a very foolish employer who would waste such skills by being inflexible.

I am now an employer myself. I find that mothers take work far more seriously than they used to. By comparison with twenty or thirty years ago, they take far less maternity leave than their forbears. It used to be normal for a first-time mother to have two or three years off when her baby was born, and lose the skills that made her such a valuable employee. Now most are back at work within twelve months with their skills bang up to date.

There are conflicting reports about the effects on our children of returning to work. Research commissioned by the Smith Institute, a Labour Party think-tank, suggested that children benefit both educationally and emotionally. It compared the children of mothers who returned to work with those of mothers who stayed at home. The evidence showed that the children of the working mothers developed better reading and mathematical skills and were happier and less aggressive – provided their mothers stayed with them until they were a year old.

However, more recent research by London University's Institute of Education claims that a lack of parental attention in the pre-school years may rob children of the qualities they need to pass tough examinations in their teens. It found that boys whose mothers went back to work before they were five were twelve per cent less likely to pass an exam at GCSE or A-level than the average. Girls suffered a ten per cent drop in their academic achievement. Full-time work is said to be more damaging than part-time work because it allows less contact between mother and child.

But crucial questions are not answered by either of these studies. The children surveyed were in their pre-school years in the early 1960s and 1970s, when, according to government statistics, there were six times fewer nurseries compared with today (Social Focus on Women 1995). The total number of day care places for the under fives was about a third of the present figures. Less than a quarter of women returned to their jobs within the first years of a child's life. They tended to be the most socially deprived and many relied on family and friends to look after their babies. Breastfeeding wasn't even considered by most mothers who were returning to work early. It was too often an amateurish, pillar-to-post approach which was bound to end in tears.

Social conditions have changed enormously. Equal opportunities policies mean it is no longer predominantly the poorest mothers who return to work while their children are very young. Good professional childcare is now much more widely available because working women are now the norm. Some options, such as paying for a first-class nanny or childminder, are, I would argue, likely to produce educational results at least as good as if the mother stays at home, provided the carer does not change too often. Even 'breastfeeding' is now possible while you are at work because you can express milk and store it in the fridge, an option not dreamed of thirty or forty years ago.

Government advice, based on the Smith Institute report, is that all working mothers should stay at home for the first year. But even here, I am not convinced that one rule can apply to all. If you can afford first-class childcare, I do not think your baby is disadvantaged if you go back to work well before his or her first birthday.

However, dumping your baby with a poor childminder or a badly-run nursery, forcing him or her to mix with toddlers who need more attention, is a recipe for a stressed and backward child. In such circumstances, it may be best to stay away from work and become a full-time mother for a year or longer, even if this means living in relative poverty. At least then you can guarantee the quality of your baby's care.

The challenge for us all is to find first-class childcare we can afford, even if it is for only part of the day. Child-minders, nannies, nurseries and pre-school playgroups can be excellent mother-substitutes, so can grandmothers or friends, provided we, as mothers, also do our share of looking after our babies every day. It may mean acquiring quite advanced juggling skills – working part-time and being mothers part-time – but, with a bit of ingenuity, most of us can do the right thing for our children and keep our self-esteem as workers. The following chapters will try to show you how.

2: THE BATTLE PLAN

A baby is Nature's way of making you get real. Forget 'having it all'. There isn't time. Compromise can no longer be a dirty word. Compromise is your new philosophy of life. There is no point in avoiding this, in pretending that you can carry on as before, with your baby as a mere designer accessory. You (and your partner) have to start with a blank sheet of paper and work out what you want from life, what you need to survive and what you can let go. You must draw up your battle plan.

You should ask yourself whether or not you like your job enough to want to carry on full-time. Would you rather work part-time so that you can spend more time with your baby? The statistics, as we have seen, show that babies thrive on the stimulation of having mum (or a first-class mother-substitute such as a nanny or a skilled childminder) on hand for the first year. A mother's or father's presence improves the child's language and mathematical skills when he or she gets older and makes for happier, less aggressive children.

Few of us can afford the luxury of staying away from work for a year. I went back to work full-time within weeks of the birth of both my sons. I did not feel I had too much choice. On both occasions, I had not been in my job long enough to qualify for the company's maternity leave and benefits package. I also knew several mothers who had taken a long time out of the office and had found it very difficult to get back into a working routine. I did not want to fall into that trap. Nor did I want anyone else to take my job. In the world of newspapers no one is indispensable. The longer you are away, the less you know about current events and the bigger the chance that a rival will stab you in the back.

Nearly seven out of ten first-time mothers return to work before their babies are a year old, and the majority reduce their working hours. More would return if employers were more 'family-friendly'. In a survey of a thousand first-time mothers in 1999, nearly three quarters said they would feel happier about going back to work if their employer offered workplace nurseries. The vast majority would take less challenging jobs if it meant they were more likely to leave on time and suffer less from work-related pressures.

A lot depends on the generosity of your employer. South Lanarkshire Council near Glasgow, for example, encourages a whole range of flexible working hours for mothers and fathers, including four-day weeks, compressed hours, job sharing, working 'at home' (clerical staff using kitchen table computers) and working 'from home' (health and safety officers who do their site visits until lunch, spend their afternoons with their children, then catch up on the paperwork after tea).

The council also runs holiday clubs during the Easter, summer and October half-term holidays for children aged five to fourteen at a cost of £10 a day for the first child and £8 for additional children. This is a godsend to mothers with older children. However, not all employers are so far-sighted, despite the evidence that 'family-friendly' policies are good for business.

Bad employers

If you work for a 'family-unfriendly' employer, however, you must plan your pregnancy and maternity leave with military precision. It is never too early to start. I began as soon as I knew I was pregnant. My boss was male and deeply chauvinist. I needed to be sure of how I would handle my childcare and working arrangements before I told him I was pregnant. I also waited until I had the amniocentesis results from the hospital before I went public.

There were so many details to work out. I had no relatives living nearby who could help with day-to-day childcare. Could I afford a full-time nanny? Would a nursery or a childminder be a better choice? How could I keep in touch with what was going on in the office during my maternity leave? How could I keep up to scratch with all the press releases and other information I needed to run my section of the paper? Could I work part-time or from home for a while?

Sex discrimination laws make it a woman's right to convert her present job to part-time employment when she has a child if it is practicable to do so. 'Family-friendly' policies are gradually becoming more widespread, particularly since European Directives on part-time work, parental leave and working hours. These will shift the balance in favour of working mothers.

But the law does not change deep-seated attitudes. A recent National Opinion Poll survey of 500 working mothers was not very encouraging. One in five women said their bosses were displeased, negative or indifferent to their pregnancies.

My boss was exactly that type. He would probably have gone purple in the face at the suggestion that an entire section of a national newspaper could be run by a three-day-a-week editor. Would he have found some ruse to replace me with a rival who did not have family commitments and was willing to work five days a week? Would I have had the nerve to take the case to court, knowing that I would still have to work with my boss if I won? And what if I lost? Would I be out of a job? I chose a live-in nanny and returned full time.

Diplomacy and fair dealing are usually more effective in dealing with an unsympathetic boss than insisting on your rights. If you approach your employer with solutions, you are more likely to get what you want. But you must do your research first.

Nicky, my hairdresser, did just that. When she told me that she was twelve weeks pregnant, she added, almost casually, that she would be returning to work for three days a week, soon after her baby was born. She would travel from her home in Essex to central London. She had already negotiated which days she would work and which days she would take off. She had arranged childcare for her three-day working week. She had sorted out most of the details with her employer before even thinking of names for her first child. She knew what she wanted and was going for it.

Your new life

Plan your broad strategy. If you want to keep your present job, should you think about moving house to make the home-childcare-work triangle smaller? This may seem like a drastic step, but you have to plan for emergencies – the days when nothing goes right. What if your car breaks down? Could you do the journey by public transport? How much would a taxi cost?

What if your child fell ill? How long would it take you to travel to the nursery, pick your child up and take him or her to an emergency carer's house, before returning to work yourself? Many new mothers find that moving closer to relatives makes emergency backup much easier to organise.

For mothers with two or more children there is an additional problem to solve – how to cope with long school holidays as well as ferrying your toddler to and from a nursery or childminder's. Children in the UK have three months' holiday a year. These can cost between £1,200 and £3,600 in extra child care payments, depending on whether you choose a childminder, a nursery or a nanny. Some employers are now offering mothers the option to work during term-time only in recognition of the difficulties caused by school holidays (see Chapter 4: Work Options).

Your relationships change when you have a baby. If you are a first-time mother, you should work out how much parenting you will do and how much will fall to your partner. Increasing numbers of partners are sharing childcare, adjusting their working hours to fit in with those of the mother. As you will read in Chapter 4, some employers are now offering wide options for men as well as women. For example, one father, a social worker, has chosen to work a four-day week. So has his wife, who works as a medical secretary. It means they have to find only three days of childcare each week instead of five.

Some couples where both partners work have a greater choice of childcare as a result. They can look for a nursery or childminder near either of their places of work. This can be crucial if one partner works in an expensive downtown area and the other has a job out of town where the cost of good childcare is lower.

A baby also affects your relationships with colleagues. This is especially true of mothers in highly-paid jobs where there can be a great deal of resentment. Your workmates may no longer regard you as a 'team player'. Your boss may not want to accommodate your new needs. Some will even try to put obstacles in your way by scheduling meetings or tasks for times when you have to pick up your child, as several mothers testify in Chapter 15: The Worker Returns.

Changing jobs

In such circumstances should you change jobs? Would a new job pay you well enough for you to afford proper childcare? Would you have to rethink your childcare to fit in with new travel arrangements?

It is very difficult to switch jobs when you are pregnant. At best, you will have only four or five months to find a new employer. You will almost certainly lose any chance of extended maternity leave since most employers insist that you should have a year's employment before you are entitled to more than the basic 18 weeks of maternity leave (see Chapter 5: Know Your Rights). Besides, it is not a good start to a new job to announce that you will soon be leaving to have a baby. How are your new colleagues supposed to react?

A better strategy is to change jobs a few months after maternity leave. That way you do not lose any company benefits. Besides, a new employer will be much more impressed if you arrive at an interview having solved the problems of working and bringing up a baby in your old job than if you are a mother-to-be with no experience of co-ordinating the two roles.

Of course, you could always take a career break. But, as you will read (Chapter 4: Work Options), this takes courage and organisation. To be successful, you must:

● plan to keep up with changes in your workplace while you are away

● be prepared to go on training courses to keep up to scratch

● keep in touch with your former colleagues so that you are not a stranger when you return.

Most of us play safe and stick with the job we have, even if it is less than perfect. At least that way we can afford to pay our bills in the short term.

Announcing your pregnancy

We can ruin our careers by bungling the way we announce our pregnancies. One in eight working mothers does not tell her boss until she is five months pregnant, according to a recent National Opinion Polls survey. Some leave it even longer, sticking to the letter of the law which allows you to leave your announcement until three weeks before the birth (see Chapter 5: Know Your Rights). But this can cause huge resentment. Being legally right does not make you popular. If you leave your company in the lurch by failing to tell them about your pregnancy until it is too late for them to plan for your absence, you cannot expect much respect on your return.

It is also an error to tell your colleagues before your boss. Employers do not like to be the last to know. They do not like to feel railroaded. It is far better to negotiate your way to your desired solution rather than to lay down the law. To dictate what you will and will not do risks not only turning your boss against you, but your colleagues as well. Jealousy and resentment are real problems in the workplace as several mothers testify.

Planning your way ahead

Before you do anything else, you must investigate your childcare options. You cannot know which hours or days you will be able to work until you have chosen the childminder, nursery, nanny, friend or relation who will look after your baby when you return. Only when you have done that can you work out how your job and your partner's job might fit your new life.

The next three chapters spell out the essential information for the battle ahead. The first step is to know what childcare is available before you even think of telling your boss about your pregnancy. Then you should know all the work options that might be available to you such as reduced hours, working only during school terms, or even taking a career break. Finally, you should swot up on your rights. If you have already made your Big Announcement, you may have left it a little late. Catch up quickly and arm yourself with the facts you need to organise your return to work.

3: CHOOSING CHILDCARE

A new-born baby needs love. A three-year-old toddler needs play.
A five-year-old child needs school.

Childcare needs alter as children grow. What never changes is the working mother's dilemma: 'How can I do the right thing by my child and be a good worker at the same time?' This is never more acute than with a first baby – especially if you are a lone parent on a low income.

In a survey in 1999, nearly a third of first-time mothers who did not return to work said they could not afford to do so because childcare cost so much. Contrast that with countries like France, where nursery places are free for all children above the age of two and of a very high standard. Eight out of ten lone mothers in France work, more than double the figure for the UK.

It is likely to take at least a decade for Britain to catch up with the rest of Europe. In the meantime, you have to choose the best childcare currently on offer and be aware of the pitfalls, especially for nurseries and nursery classes. It is not merely a question of sorting good from bad, but choosing the most appropriate care for the age of your child.

New-born babies

The first twelve months of a child's life are crucial. All the evidence shows that if a baby is deprived of motherly love at this early stage in its development, it will suffer both emotionally and educationally.

But motherly love can come from more than one source, as extended families all over the world prove every day. Your duty as a first-time working mother is either to take time off to nurture your baby through its first year (suffering loss of income and possibly damaging your career prospects), or find ways of creating your own extended family by hiring good professional help and enlisting trusted friends and relatives who will cherish and feed your little mite while you are away.

The options for new-born babies are related to their needs. They need warmth, security, hygiene and mother's milk. Not so long ago, the latter could only have been supplied by the mother herself (or, in the case of rich families, by a hired wet nurse). In the past, mothers had to put up with offering their children shop-bought 'baby milk' as a substitute for the real thing. But we now live in the age of refrigeration and electric breast pumps. Mother's milk can be stored and given to your child by someone else such as your partner, the baby's grandfather or a professional child-carer.

This is important. It means you have new freedoms denied to working mothers in previous generations. Expressing milk using a breast pump may be a chore, especially when you do it in the ladies' loo at work, but it allows you a real choice. You do not have to stay at home. Nor do you have to feel guilty. If you find a good carer to act as a mother-substitute, you will not be depriving your child in any way, particularly if you nurture your baby every day when you finish work.

However, some kinds of childcare – some day nurseries for example – may be unsuitable for babies because your child will not receive enough individual attention. You must find a proper mother-substitute instead, someone who will nurture your baby as you would if you did not return to work. Unless you work from home, you have four main options – nannies, members of your family, childminders or a nursery with a dedicated baby room.

Children aged two to five

By the age of two, a child needs to get out and play. Socialising with other children is important. A great deal of research shows that high-quality nursery education with play at its core, led by qualified staff with early years training on child development, is the best foundation you can give your child.

If you lived in France, you would have no problems. Nursery education is free for every child over the age of two. The staff are generally better qualified than their British equivalents and they have high status in their communities. Large amounts of money are spent on buildings and equipment.

Here, there are far too few nurseries to go round – around seven thousand at the last count catering for a mere quarter of a million children up to the age of eight. The quality of nurseries is patchy, too. Local authority nurseries and some hospital nurseries are never inspected because of a loophole in the law. Some are very badly managed. A few private nurseries attached to schools are bad too, allowing large numbers of two-year-olds to be supervised by very few staff.

In the options set out below you will find out how to avoid choosing a bad nursery and how to opt for an alternative. Some working mothers should avoid nurseries altogether. To take an extreme example, a surgeon with children aged three and four cannot stop in the middle of an operation because her children need picking up from the nursery at six o'clock. She needs much more flexible childcare. But what should it be – a nanny, a mother's help, an au pair, a childminder or something else?

Mothers who work from home have new options. If you are a 'teleworker', for example, you might be able to keep an eye on your children by supervising an unqualified carer in your home, while you sit at your computer in the corner. You delegate your responsibilities, but you are still in charge and you can intervene whenever necessary. Again, you need to know all the options and decide which comes closest to your ideal.

School-age children

Childcare problems for a working mother do not end when your child is five. They just get more complicated, especially if you have younger children, too. The school day seems to be designed to be as inconvenient as possible. It starts too late for you to get to work by nine unless your office or factory is next door to the school. It ends in the middle of the afternoon when you are likely to be at your busiest.

This means that you must either work part time, enlist help from family or friends, or hire professional help. Those lucky enough to have the use of an after-school club may have professional help on tap. The rest of us have to muddle through. Is an au pair waiting at the school gate the answer? Why not combine a cleaner with a child-carer? What can you afford? What should you avoid?

Childcare: the ten main options

There are ten main choices of childcare. Not all will suit your family or employment circumstances. Some offer only a few hours of childcare every day. Others offer comprehensive care to allow you to return to work full time. You must choose which works best on your budget for your age of child.

1. Childminders – home childcare on a budget

Childminders are the most popular form of childcare among working mothers in Britain. More than a third of a million of us use them because they are flexible in their working hours, relatively affordable and because some nurseries do not take children until they are three years old. They are cheaper than nannies and can offer the same kind of personal care.

However, their numbers have declined during the last decade as nurseries have equipped themselves to take younger children (some now offer places to babies as young as two months), but there has been recent government encouragement for childminders to become better trained, an attempt to professionalise them and give them higher status and pay.

Childminders usually look after your children in their own homes. They are self-employed. They must be registered with their local authority, but this does not mean that they have had formal training in childcare. A few local authorities now insist that they go on pre-registration courses, but these are often no more than eight hours' worth of tuition spread over four weeks.

If you have to work late, a childminder may be willing to extend the collection time to accommodate you. On the other hand, if a childminder falls ill, you have to carry the can because there is no-one else to take over. A childminder may also refuse to look after a child who falls ill because she is afraid of infecting the other children. You must make sure you know what is expected of you if your child is sick and negotiate overtime payments if the childminder is willing to work longer hours in emergencies.

You must make your own judgements about any childminder.

- Do you trust and like her?
- Do you agree with her views on childcare?
- Have you seen references from other parents who have used her services?
- Have you taken up those references? If your baby is less than a year old, you should phone other mothers who used the childminder when their baby was the same age.

Inspection

Childminders are vetted by the police and social services at the time of registration to make sure they are 'fit' to look after children. This vetting procedure also applies to everyone else in the childminder's household who is over 16, including the childminder's older children.

The childminder's premises must be inspected every year by the local social services department, but in many areas of the country, this is a very hit-and-miss system, with standards of inspection for some areas relatively poor. Inspection will very soon become the responsibility of a national team under the auspices of OFSTED, the schools' inspectorate, which will regulate childcare and education outside the home for every child from the age of three months.

Disadvantages

A childminder has sole charge of your child, so there is no-one else to see how well she copes. You have to make your own judgements. If you, or someone you trust, get the chance to arrive unannounced, you can make an assessment on the spot.

If a childminder has a young family herself, all her own children have to be counted in and she is not allowed to take more than the allowed limits (see Rules, below). This can make some childminders dependent on a single family for their livelihood.

Blackmailed by her childminder: *Daisy had a tough job in a big multinational company. She often had to work 55 hours a week at peak times of the year. Her husband worked even longer hours. They were hardly seeing their children, eighteen-month-old Caroline and five-year-old Spike, except at weekends.*

Daisy was desperate to go part-time, but she had another responsibility – her childminder, a single mother with four children to support. Daisy was her sole customer. She employed her for 50 hours a week which gave the childminder an income of £640 a month. If Daisy went part-time, the childminder's income would drop by almost £200.

'I felt I was affecting her family income by reducing my work pattern, and it was a barrier which prevented me from pursuing the part-time option for quite a long time, because I felt quite a responsibility to her. The income I was giving her was keeping her family going and I knew she had no support from her husband financially. But in the end we had to say our family comes first and I renegotiated a contract with our childminder.

'I could have changed childminders and let her take on some other children full-time, but my little girl is very sensitive about who she spends

time with. It took me six weeks to get her used to my current childminder, and I was very loath to change because I believe childcare should be about continuity. Caroline screamed every day for weeks and to go through that again would have been hell on earth.

'Both my children were under five and her youngest was two years old so the maximum she was allowed to mind was two children under five. I really went through battling with my conscience, I lost sleep over this because I felt I was doing somebody else out of an income and I felt it wasn't right. It took me quite a while to get through that. My friends said I must consider my own family first.'

Advantages

The advantage of a childminder over a nursery or a nanny is often continuity of care. It is not unusual for a childminder to look after the same children for three years or more.

Childminders as extended family: *Sue had only two childminders in eight years. When her daughter Rebecca was born, she gave up work for thirteen months, then took a weekend job at a department store. Her husband took over the childcare then. When her son Thomas was born, Rebecca was four. She found a childminder who could take Rebecca to school and look after Thomas during the day. A year later, she took a full-time job, the start of a career which led to her becoming the general manager of two department stores.*

'They were proper childminders' said Sue. 'After school when they'd had their tea they'd get the paints out and they would do pictures and go on nature trails and collect leaves and do abstract pictures and lots of other things. One had a husband who was a policeman. He worked shifts so he was able to give them some sort of male presence as well, in a family environment. It worked very well.

The first childminder had Thomas until he went to school at five, then she wanted another full-time child. The second childminder lasted until my daughter went to senior school. I've been very lucky. It's better than leaving them with auntie or grandmother often. That can work, but I felt they were with someone who was a similar age to me, had a young family as well and devoted her time to them and included them as part of the family. A grandmother might not do as much, she might just sit them in front of the telly. No disrespect for grandmothers but some of them do.'

Rules

● A childminder can look after no more than three children under the age of five and three children aged five to eight. This includes her own children.

● There is no legal limit on the number of children older than eight who can be cared for by a childminder before or after school and during school holidays. Some local authorities suggest a total of ten children as a maximum for one childminder.

● Premises have to be classified as 'fit' under the Children Act of 1989. They must comply with health and safety regulations, and each childminder must keep records of each child and have a record of local emergency numbers and each child's special medication or health problems.

● Some local authorities make special conditions about premises. Cheshire, for example, recently insisted that no childminder could have a garden pond unless it was covered with a metal grid of a specified type and bolted to the ground.

The village childminder: *'I had to do quite a lot of work in my kitchen before they'd let me look after other people's children,' says Jenny, a childminder in a village of 120 people near Malton in North Yorkshire. She bought the semi-detached house next to her own to give her enough space to cater for the village children. She knocked the two main rooms into one and has fenced off an area in the garden next to the house so that toddlers can play outside while she keeps an eye on them from inside. The local council visited her home to make sure that it complied with regulations.*

Jenny began her job when her own girls were six and seven years old and well-established at the school in the next village. Her workload varies. 'I look after two children on Mondays, three on Tuesdays and then usually one the rest of the week. I also look after a little girl who comes after school. I need at least two children to make the job pay.

'I let the older ones watch 'Playbus' and 'Pippin' on the television because they're educational and good. But I don't let them watch satellite TV because it's not a high enough standard. Childminding suits me. I like to be at home and I don't have to have a car, which is a big saving, really.'

Finding and choosing a childminder

One of the reasons childminders' numbers have declined is the difficulty mothers face in finding them. Only one in a hundred companies helps its workers to find a childminder according to a Government survey in 1996. A few, like the cosmetics firm Elida Fabergé in Leeds, co-operate with the local authority to recommend childminders to their workers. But even this can lead to difficulties. Childminders can only take a set number of children. If they are in demand because they have been recommended by a company or by word of mouth, they have to turn parents away. It may be a year before a vacancy with a popular childminder crops up. It is therefore important to look early in your pregnancy, at least six months before you need their services.

Your council's social services department will have a list of childminders. You should choose ones near your home or your workplace and pay them a visit. It is worth asking the officer in charge of local inspections for tips. Ring for an appointment before you visit. The inspector may steer you clear of childminders who will not suit your preferences. That done, you should visit the childminders in person and see several before choosing.

It is up to you to judge the mix of children in the care of each childminder. Toddlers tend to take up much more of a childminder's time because they are constantly getting into danger. Too many toddlers and your baby may be neglected.

Many mothers use childminders to fill in the gaps before and after school.

Close to home: *Lone parent Sara has her seven-year-old daughter Amy collected from school by a childminder two days a week while she works nearby as a full-time senior supervisor at the Cheshire Health Agency. She leaves her two-year-old son Matthew with the same childminder for three days a week. Her mother covers the other days. 'It works really well,' she says. 'The childminder, my mum and the school are all within two hundred yards of each other.'*

Cost

The cost varies greatly from one part of the country to another. You must negotiate face-to-face.

- Usually the least you can expect to pay is between £1.50 and £2 an hour. For fifty hours of cover (8am-6pm), this comes to £75 to £100 a week. Some childminders will look after babies at discount rates – as little as £1 an hour.

● The most you can expect to pay is £4 an hour, usually in big cities where property prices are high. For 50 hours of cover (8am-6pm), this comes to £200 a week

● You should reach an agreement for the payment of overtime in emergencies. This is often 'time and a half'. If you are paying £2.50 an hour during the day, you can expect to pay £3.75 an hour for overtime.

2. Nannies – mother-substitutes at a price

Nannies come in four varieties, live-in and live-out, qualified and unqualified. You pay more for live-out nannies because they have to pay for their own accommodation. You pay more for qualified nannies because they have specialist skills, particularly with young babies. All are in demand and you should allow at least three months to find one.

Historical background

Britain has the best nannies in the world, partly because ours is the only country to train them systematically in home childcare and partly because we have never adequately funded alternatives such as free or heavily-subsidised nursery provision. In France, for example, nursery care is free to all from the age of two. Ten times more children are in publicly-funded daycare compared with the UK. Twice as many lone parents return to work.

The British system of nanny training is a by-product of our former class divisions. Poor and middle-income families in the UK were traditionally expected to look after their own children. Wealthy families, by contrast, had access to excellent childcare – an army of uniformed nannies trained at colleges such as Norland and Princess Christian. Such families had homes big enough for nannies to live in. Nannies were status symbols.

Those days have gone. Now a nanny is much more likely to be employed by an ordinary working mother. Many nannies are shared by two families. Nannies no longer wear uniforms; they are usually regarded as part of the family and expect to be treated as such. By historical accident, therefore, Britain has inherited a genuinely good (if rather costly) way of caring for our children while we work.

Advantages

The huge advantage of a nanny is that she works from your home (or the home of the other family in a nanny-share in which you team up with another mother and split the costs). If your child falls ill, she is there to provide nursing care. Unlike a nursery or a childminder, you do not have to leave work to attend to every emergency. She is a true mother-substitute.

A nanny is much more flexible in her working hours than a childminder, nursery or a workplace creche. With negotiation, she can adjust her hours to fit yours. Most nannies are very willing to do this, providing they can predict when they have time off so that they, like you, can organise a social life.

Morning routines are much simpler with a nanny. You do not have to get your baby up, dressed and fed before you go to work. You can lead a near-normal working life, especially if the nanny lives in your house.

Disadvantages

However, loss of privacy is a serious problem for some mothers. They do not like the idea of a stranger in their own home. Nannies have friends. They have social lives to live. They alter the balance of your household.

Boyfriend at work: *'I came home early and found her sitting on the sofa with her boyfriend,' said Sue, who works as a high-powered secretary in central London. 'She said her boyfriend had just called in to say hello, but I couldn't be sure how long he had been there. The baby was asleep in her room, and the baby monitor was switched on, but I didn't feel she had her mind on the job.'*

Sue laid down a rule that boyfriends could only visit outside working hours or by pre-arrangement and they were not allowed to stay overnight. The cut-off time was 11pm. She also insisted that the nanny was home by midnight whenever she had a night out in the working week.

'It was really difficult,' she said, 'because I felt like the nanny's mother, laying down rules about what she could and couldn't do. It created quite a bit of tension at first, because my home was her home, too. But in the end, I was paying her to do a job. Her private life should have been kept separate.'

Most employers end up making similar rules, barring boyfriends but allowing other nannies to visit with the children in their charge, for example. Then they have to make more rules to stop the visiting nannies eating them out of house and home.

The greedy nannies: *'They almost doubled my food bill,' complained Sarah, an American banker who employed a live-in nanny to look after her two children, Ben and Amy. 'She would invite the other nannies round for coffee in the morning and they would stay for lunch. It was always my house they chose, because my nanny was pretty outgoing.'*

'It was great for the kids because they could play together, but eventually I had to put a limit on the amount of entertaining. The last straw was when I cooked a turkey for Thanksgiving and the nannies helped themselves.'

Rules

Here are the golden rules to stop live-in nannies overstepping the mark.

- Set aside a shelf in the fridge and freezer which is out of bounds to the nanny or label food so that she knows not to use it. Likewise, get her to label food she has bought and wants for herself.
- Establish a 'house wallet' which the nanny can use for buying food, groceries and outings with your children. Make sure she puts in receipts for everything she buys. If you mostly use one grocery store, consider giving your nanny a charge card for that store.
- Share shopping lists to avoid duplication. Make sure your list includes your nanny's special food needs.
- Establish a fair-share system for the telephone. For example, the nanny can make local calls of a certain length free. Charge your nanny for long-distance calls or any local calls which are longer than the agreed limit. Make her justify any unauthorised telephone calls when the itemised bill arrives.
- Establish the rules for using your car. For example, the nanny should pay for all the parking tickets she receives. The nanny should ask before using your car in the evening (so that you know where it is if anything goes wrong). The nanny should not allow your children to travel in other nannies' cars without your permission.
- Spell out the limits for socialising, such as a midnight curfew for weekdays so that your live-in nanny is not disturbing the household when she returns from a night out and so that she gets enough sleep to be fit for work. If she does not work at weekends, ask her where she is staying overnight, so that you know where to call if an emergency, such as a family crisis, occurs.

- Decide whether or not you will allow her friends to stay overnight. Make sure she invites them only with permission.
- Agree on how loud the nanny is allowed to play music in her room.
- Set aside times when she can use the washing machine for her own laundry, preferably during her working hours so that she does not prevent you washing your own clothes.
- If you are worried about your child's diet or behaviour, ask your nanny to start a Baby Diary which lists when the baby was asleep, awake, playing or crying and what the baby eats during each day.
- Do not install spy cameras to check up on your nanny. This is a gross invasion of her privacy and indicates that you have no trust. With the invention of 'web cameras' it is reasonable to place one in your child's room so that you can take a look during the day. However, you must let your nanny know where the camera is.
- Draw up a contract listing full details of working hours, overtime pay, duties and periods of notice. This is a legal obligation. You must do so within eight weeks of the start of a nanny's employment.

On the following page is a (very) fictional example of what one might look like based on the characters in the Walt Disney movie *Mary Poppins*. The overall shape and content of this contract gives you a good idea of the kinds of things you must include. You need to cover the general ground of duties, pay, hours of work, holidays and 'sackable offences'. It is up to you to define what these are. Indeed most of the categories are negotiable. If the nanny does not like them, she will not sign and you will have to find someone else.

CONTRACT OF EMPLOYMENT

*Mary Poppins is employed by George and Winifred Banks of Eaton Square, Belgravia,
as nanny to their children, Jane and Michael. Her duties start on January 1st.*

Duties: To care for the children during working hours on a sole charge basis. To dress
them, make their meals, feed them, wash them, toilet them and supervise their play.
To launder their clothes. To shop for their food and other daily needs. To accompany
them on outings when required. To accompany the family on holidays. To drive the
children in the family car to events as directed by Mr or Mrs Banks.

Hours of work: Basic hours 7.30am to 5pm Monday to Friday inclusive during the
working year. Overtime is paid at a separate rate and is voluntary by mutual agreement
between employee and employers (advance warning of 48 hours whenever possible).
During family holidays, hours of work are 7.30am to midnight Monday to Saturday
inclusive subject to voluntary agreement to opt out of the maximum 48-hour week as
set out in the European Working Time Directive.

Holidays: Four weeks' paid holiday per year (timing to be agreed with employers) plus
public holidays.

Notice: Four weeks, in writing, by either employer or employee.

Pay:
- Basic weekly pay (after tax and National Insurance is paid by employer) £350
- Overtime pay ....£8 per hour
- Weekly holiday pay £400
- Sick pay for the first two weeks of illness or injury £350
- Sick pay after the first two weeks of illness or injury £100
- Time limit for sick pay – three months after the onset of illness or injury
- Expenses – any spending for the benefit of the children to be agreed in advance by the
employers and paid for by them.

Sackable offences
Smacking the children
Smoking while on duty
Staying out beyond midnight during the working week
Allowing friends to stay in her room overnight without permission
Sexual misconduct while on duty
Putting the children at physical or psychological risk
Singing songs with chimney sweeps
Performing magic tricks detrimental to the children's welfare (such as leading them up
smoke staircases into the sky)

Signed   *Date*

Mary Poppins_____   _____

George Banks_____   _____

Winifred Banks_____   _____

Regulation

Nannies are entirely unregulated. Unlike childminders and nurseries, there is no local register or annual inspection because they work in your home. Recent attempts to establish a national register failed through lack of Government support. It was argued that a register would be unworkable and unreliable. How could inspectors keep track of nannies who changed jobs every six months? How could they enforce minimum standards of safety in ordinary homes? How could standards of care be policed when nannies worked alone with only the mother or father to monitor their work? A monster to one employer may seem a saint to another. A nanny with a string of qualifications may be a hopeless carer. A nanny with no qualifications may be loving and capable. A mother who employs a nanny, therefore, must use her own judgement.

I would argue that you should have 'state-registered nannies' in the same way as you have 'state-registered nurses'. It would depend, however on establishing a professional body with the powers to strike off any nanny who was in serious breach of an established code of conduct. Such de-registration could only take place if the professional body had quasi-judicial powers and had a disciplinary procedure with the backing of law. It would have to be fair to the accused nanny. There may even have to be a right to legal representation.

Registered nannies might expect to earn more than those who did not belong to the professional body. However, if the difference in pay was too great, their professional status might price them out of the market. This would be counter-productive. It would drive parents into choosing unregistered nannies on cost grounds.

In the meantime, the Government is setting up a voluntary code of practice for nanny agencies and may award 'quality assurance' symbols to those which comply. In future this should mean that:

- All agencies are inspected by government officials.
- Agencies which breach 'good practice' guidelines will be shut down.
- All nannies listed by agencies will have been interviewed face to face.
- The identity of all nannies listed by an agency will have been checked.
- The nannies' right to work will have been verified.
- The nannies' qualifications will have been verified.
- The nannies' work history will have been checked.
- The nannies' references will have been verified and assessed.
- The nannies' suitability for specific employers will have been assessed.

(for example, if you specifically request a non-smoker, you should be offered a nanny who does not smoke).

There has been no government statement about police checks on nannies. Local authorities ask for police checks on all childminders to ensure that they do not have criminal records for sexual offences or the physical abuse of children. The same should apply to nannies. However, it is unclear if nanny agencies will have any right to obtain police checks on nannies who apply to be on their lists. This is vital if men, in particular, are to be considered as nannies. Parents need reassurance that they are not employing paedophiles. At the moment, many good male nannies are being unfairly discriminated against because of the absence of proper checks.

There have been recent disturbing claims by the Professional Association of Nursery Nurses that some parents are trying to cut the pay of nannies by insisting that they call themselves 'au pairs' or 'mothers' helps'. Some parents are said to have sacked nannies before they are 21 to avoid paying the minimum wage. If this is true, it is not only illegal, it also undermines all the attempts to professionalise nannies by establishing minimum standards of pay for minimum qualifications.

Qualifications

A fully-qualified nanny has genuine expertise in spotting symptoms of illness and taking appropriate action. She will have been trained in safe, good nutrition and the best methods of monitoring your child's wellbeing. She will have learned about the early years of child development. She will be able to give your child the same attention you would give if you were not working. She can be left in sole charge.

You should check a nanny's qualifications. There are three recognised schemes. The most prestigious is NVQ Level 3 (formerly NNEB), which involves a two year full-time nursery nursing course with two days' practical experience a week. A BTEC is a nursery nursing diploma from a college awarded by the Business and Technical Education Council. An NAMCW is a nursery nursing diploma awarded by the National Association for Maternal and Child Welfare.

However, no qualification can tell you whether a nanny is kind or well-organised. You must make that judgement yourself by observing her in action. As with all carers left in sole charge of a child, the only way to tell (short of using spy cameras) is to make a few visits unannounced.

Unqualified nannies are not usually a good choice for new-born babies. They may be organised, outgoing and loving but they do not have the grounding in child development and modern medical theory that training involves. A thorough knowledge of a baby's needs is as important as common sense and a caring personality.

However, when your children get older, unqualified nannies may be preferable because they often have more experience of life. One of the best nannies I employed was a British-Canadian marine biology graduate who had left her home town of Toronto to find her family roots. She was clever, funny, had her own flat and friends and made my children's lives much richer.

Finding a nanny

Finding a nanny can be expensive and time-consuming in itself. A single advertisement in such London-based publications as '*The Lady*' or '*Nursery World*' will cost you around £100.

You can contact a nanny recruitment agency, but fees of £300–£600 are not unusual and there is no guarantee of quality until the Government's so-called 'quality assurance' scheme is properly established. The childcare minister, Margaret Hodge, recently described nanny agencies as 'ghastly'. She said: 'They just get names of nannies and make a fortune in turning them around.'

You can also write or telephone colleges of further education and dedicated nursery nurse training schools such as Norland College in Berkshire. However, it is worth sounding a note of caution if you have a new-born baby. You may need a more experienced nanny than a raw NVQ Level 3 graduate can offer. The National Childbirth Trust (020 8992 8637) will give you excellent advice on finding a nanny to suit your needs.

Cost

The biggest drawback of nannies is the cost, especially if you have only one child. Live-in nannies are paid £250–£300 a week in London after tax and National Insurance. Realistically, this means you would have to earn up to £500 a week before tax to cover your costs. Outside London and the other big cities, nannies earn far less; £150–£200 a week for a live-in nanny is typical.

Live-out nannies are more expensive still – up to £350 a week in London and up to £250 elsewhere. They usually cost less in terms of expenses such as food and telephone bills. They tend to be older, with homes and social lives of their own. A typical arrangement might be for a live-out nanny to arrive at eight in the morning and leave at six in the evening. You need to negotiate overtime rates for late working and decide on the notice needed to qualify for such a service – usually 36 or 48 hours – so that the nanny can plan her social life around it.

It is usual that you pay both the employer's and the employee's tax contributions. In addition, as an employer of a live-in nanny you should meet her heating, food and telephone costs – within limits which you have to lay down. It is not reasonable, for example, for a nanny to expect you to pay for her trans-Atlantic calls to her boyfriend. It is reasonable, however, for you to pay for her local calls, since many of those relate to work. Chatting to other nannies on the telephone is vital if she is to organise a social life for your child.

An employer is expected to pay the nanny's transport costs while she is at work. This varies from buying season tickets for public transport to the use of a car. In good times, some qualified nannies in the big cities can virtually name their own perks – a separate flat, their own car, weekends off guaranteed. There is always someone rich enough to pay for it. Luckily, most nannies are much more reasonable in their demands.

Interview checklist
The interview is where your instincts come into play. But you must be methodical. You should ask:
- How long is she is prepared to stay? (surprisingly few lie about this)
- What is her family background? (nannies with strong families tend to be more stable)
- What were her previous nannying jobs?
- Why did she leave?
- Why are there gaps on her CV (it could mean she was fired and doesn't want you to know).
- What does she know about first aid and safety precautions?
- What are her attitudes to discipline?
- What activities does she enjoy doing with children?
- What does she enjoy cooking?
- Does she smoke?
- Does she have a boyfriend? (and does he live at the other end of the country?)

- What does she like to do in her time off?
- What references does she have from previous employers? (You should telephone at least two of the nanny's referees to see if her story checks out. This is vital for your own peace of mind.)

In eleven years, I have never employed a bad nanny, partly because my partner and I always took up references and talked to the nannies' previous employers. The nearest we have had to a problem was one fully-qualified nanny who was far too quiet.

That is not to say that we did not interview (and reject) some poor child-carers. But they were relatively easy to spot – the disco queens, the non-English speakers, the nervous types, the easily-led, the ones with no references. References are vital and more important than qualifications.

One mother rang me for a reference on a nanny I had employed for two years. She asked question after question. I told her the girl was brilliant, reliable and outgoing. She still seemed unsure. What was the problem? She confessed that she had recently employed a nanny without telephoning the girl's previous employers. It was a mistake. The nanny had a criminal boyfriend who persuaded her to let him use the employer's car for a ramraid on a warehouse. The nanny went along too.

Nannyshares
If the idea of a nanny sounds too expensive, but you still want the convenience such first-class childcare can offer, you have only one option – to share a nanny with a friend who has a child roughly the same age as your own. This is a variation on child-minding since it will almost certainly mean that you have to take your child to your friend's house some of the time. Many mothers alternate houses week by week to make it fair. Some live-out nannies are prepared to call at your house first and take your baby to the other house, thus saving you the trouble of a journey.

A nanny-share is not usually as cheap as a childminder if you only have one child. You can expect to pay around £150 a week in London and other big cities and around £120 a week elsewhere. Only you know whether you can afford it, or whether the extra convenience is worth it.

3. Mother's Helps – housekeepers who care
A mother's help is someone you hire to help you with your household chores and assist you in looking after your children. She is not trained

in childcare and should not be left in sole charge of a pre-school child. A first-time mother should not employ a mother's help unless she plans to stay at home and look after her baby herself.

This means that mother's helps are most useful to mothers with school-age children. They do tasks such as cleaning, shopping, cooking and collecting children from school. If a mother's help lives in your spare room, she may be called a 'housekeeper'. Most, however, work by coming to a mother's home every day.

Some mothers limit the tasks of a mother's help to a few hours a day – an arrangement which can suit both parties very well. For example, a student may have lectures in the morning and be looking for a job in the afternoons to help her pay her fees. She will pick up your children from school and supervise them until you return from work. She will also cook their evening meal. If she has time, she may be able to pick up shopping on the way home. During the school holidays (roughly the same as college holidays) she may be able to work full-time, allowing you to continue working as normal.

This is a low-cost option which can work well, particularly if you share the cost with another mother. In big cities such as London, mother's helps are paid between £6 and £8 an hour; outside London the cost is between £4 and £6 an hour. A 15-hour working week (three hours a day) will therefore cost between £60 and £120.

Mother's helps do not have to register with the local authority. If you want to employ one to have sole charge of your children every day after school, you must make your own judgement of their abilities, and check out their references, especially those which apply to childcare.

Interview checklist

You should apply some of the same interview techniques as for a nanny:
- What are her attitudes to discipline?
- How much does she know about first-aid?
- Does she smoke?
- What sort of activities would she plan to do with the children every day?
- What would she cook for them?
- What sort of family background does she have?
- What does she do in her time off?

It may be only a three-hour-a-day job you are offering, but the checks should be much the same as if it were for eight hours. You can find

mother's helps by advertising in local newspapers and magazines.
Some nanny agencies also have them on their books. Also look in the
windows of local newsagents to see if someone living locally is looking
for that kind of work.

4. Au pairs – useful foster daughters

Au pairs are usually young students of English who live with a
family to learn something of the language and culture of a new
country. There are about 25,000 of them staying with British families
at any one time. Many study at local colleges. Their duties are to
help look after the children and to do tasks such as cleaning, shopping
and cooking.

They are not alternatives to nannies. They have no training in
childcare. Most are in their late teens or early twenties. Their lack of
experience means they must not be left in sole charge of babies.

Au pairs are very much cheaper to employ than nannies. Most
earn around £40 per week and therefore do not need to pay tax and
National Insurance. They are not covered by the national minimum
wage because the British government decided in February 2000 after
'wide public consultation' that it was wrong to classify them as
workers. Lobby groups had argued that au pairs were involved in
'cultural exchange' because they came to learn English.

An au pair's duties are to *help* a mother with domestic chores and
childcare, not to be a mother-substitute. She should not be expected to
do much more than half a day's work every day and she is entitled to
'reasonable leave and rest' under the European Working Time Directive.

However, with more mothers working from home, the dividing
lines of responsibility are becoming blurred. If, for example, a mother is
teleworking from a computer in the corner of the sitting room, she may
be able to supervise an au pair at the same time. The responsibility for
the child is still down to the mother, however. She should never leave
the au pair to cope with a pre-school child alone.

School duties

Most mothers employ au pairs to help look after older children. They
can, for example, pick up the children from school and, if their language
is good enough, supervise their after-school activities and do a few
hours of babysitting until the mother returns from work. They might
even fit in a bit of shopping or cleaning.

With older children, it is also possible to have an au pair get your children up in the morning and take them to school while you make your journey to work. This suits many au pairs who can then travel to their language courses immediately afterwards.

An au pair should be treated more like a foster child than an employee. You should give parental guidance and help her to meet friends of her own age. It is likely that you will have to arrange a language course for her with your local authority or with a private language school. The cost of such language teaching, however, is not your responsibility. Learning a language can work two ways. If you choose the nationality of your au pair to fit your children's studies, it may be possible for them to be taught a foreign language by the au pair.

Problems

Lack of English can severely hamper an au pair's usefulness. If she cannot understand what your children are saying, or cannot make herself understood, she will have little control. With older children, this can be a real problem.

The non-English speaker: *'It was a nightmare,' said Jenny, a personnel officer from Derby and the mother of two boys aged eleven and eight. 'I would come home from work and find that no homework had been done, which was the whole point of having an au pair in the first place. The children were often totally out of control. She was French and had such poor English that she could not tell the children what to do. They just ignored her and played. She was very upset because she felt such a failure, so I ended up comforting her and supervising the children's homework myself.'*

Another problem is teenage rebellion. Susan, who works as a nurse in Manchester, employed an 18-year-old Finnish au pair called Johanna to help her look after her nine-year-old son, Marcus.

The raver: *'Her English was excellent,' she said. 'You could easily have mistaken her for an English girl. The problem was that she wanted to go out every night. She was attractive and very popular. I was constantly having to call her on her mobile phone to ask her where she was and when she would be home. It was a great worry. I was having to act like her mother. After a couple of months I had to send her back to Finland because I felt she was getting into real danger.'*

Susan would not have accepted Johanna as an au pair if she had been given the chance to interview her before she came.

Agencies

Unfortunately, few agencies arrange interviews. Au pairs are simply allocated and the first you know of their personality is when they arrive. Nor do they usually stay long. Six months to a year is the best you can expect. Again, this can cause upset. No sooner have your children become fond of an au pair than she is gone.

However, a good au pair with a reasonable command of English and a mature outlook can mean the difference between working and staying at home for mothers with older children. If all she does is take the children to school and bring them home when lessons have finished, she may be worth all the heartache and worry.

Your local Yellow Pages directory usually has au pair agencies listed under 'Nanny and childcare agencies.' Some foreign churches with offshoots in Britain also arrange au pair contacts. For a full list of au pair agencies you can contact:

The Federation of Recruitment and Employment Services
36–38 Mortimer Street
London W1N 7RB
020 7323 4300

Rules

Au pairs from a country outside the EC are subject to strict controls. They must apply for a special Home Office visa which lays down the following rules:

- A maximum five hours' work per day
- No more than 25 hours a week
- A maximum two years' stay
- Compulsory free board and lodging
- A reasonable weekly allowance (no minimum wage enforced)
- Two full days off per week

5. Nurseries – sociable but inflexible

Britain's nursery provision is a national scandal. There is far too little of it. Standards are hopelessly inconsistent. Public nurseries, run by local authority social services departments or by government institutions such as hospitals, have places for about one child in a hundred and they usually ration each place to those 'at risk' or whose family has some kind of deprivation. Until new laws come into force, they do not have to be inspected and management practices are sometimes very poor. Private nurseries, which include those run by community groups and workplace 'creches', are inspected annually, but are often costly. As with all 'group provision' of childcare, nursery employees are only subjected to police checks if their individual nursery requests it – unlike childminders who must have police checks to make sure they do not have convictions for offences against children.

The Family Policy Studies Centre says that British childcare costs are the highest in Europe. In France and Belgium, all children have access to free nursery care from the age of two. The standards of staff training are much higher than in Britain. In Germany, more than half the children attend subsidised state nurseries.

Which children are suited

Nurseries are most valuable to working mothers with regular nine-to-five jobs who have children aged two to five. However, there is an increasing trend for nurseries to take children as young as two months, setting aside a 'baby room' for them.

Unless a nursery has special provision for babies, it is of little use to mothers of very young children. For reasons of cost only a few nurseries take babies: they must employ one adult for every three children under the age of two. But there is a more compelling reason. Many mothers dislike nurseries for very young children because they are often noisy places where staff have to spend a disproportionate amount of time with the more demanding older children – the toddlers who can move and talk. Unless there is space set aside and staff dedicated to baby-care, very young children can lose out in such an environment.

A baby does best in a place of relative calm – such as your home, where he or she can be monitored constantly by an adult who will offer comfort whenever it is required. Mothers who stay at home can do this. So can nannies and, to a lesser extent, childminders.

Advantages and disadvantages

In a nursery, your child will have lots of playmates, many more than a childminder can offer, and more than even the most sociable nanny can organise. With a nursery, socialising is built in.

Another big advantage of a nursery is the continuity of care. Nannies and childminders need holidays; nurseries do not. If they have enough staff to cover, they can stay open all year. Likewise, nurseries do not close because one member of staff has fallen ill. If a nanny or a childminder has an accident or an illness requiring time off, you have to carry the can.

However, nurseries can be inflexible in their opening hours and their tolerance of your emergencies at work. They are more impersonal, especially if they look after large numbers of children. They cannot cope with illness which might affect the other children in their care. In similar circumstances, a nanny will simply put the child to bed or take him or her to the see the doctor. A nursery (and most childminders) will ask you to leave work and take your child home. Above all, the more pre-school age children you have, the more expensive a nursery becomes by comparison with the alternatives. A nanny costs the same if she is looking after three children or one. A nursery demands three fees for three children.

Nurseries usually offer much better play facilities than you could have at home – sandpits, slides, paints, books and soft areas on a scale beyond a normal house. If the nursery is privately run, facilities should also be safe because the premises are inspected by the local authority every year. Most local authority nurseries are also inspected.

Choosing the nursery's location
If you live a long way from work, you might be wise to choose a nursery near your workplace, so that you can pick up your child quickly at the end of the day. This is even more important for medical emergencies. If the nursery is round the corner from work, you can pop in and check things out. A false alarm will not disrupt your working day too badly. If your child is genuinely ill, you might even be allowed to bring your child into work for an hour or so.

The downside of choosing a nursery near your work is that your child has to spend a long time travelling with you every day. If you use public transport, this can be very stressful for you both. Choosing a nursery near home gets round this problem, but you must organise local backup to cope with medical emergencies during the day. Someone must be able to pick up your child at short notice if illness strikes, or you will have to make the long journey yourself, while your colleagues pick up the pieces.

Nursery regulations

All nurseries must comply with the Children Act of 1989. They must have adult:child ratios of:

● 1:3 for children up to the age of two

● 1:4 for children from the age of two up to the age of three

● 1:8 for children from three up to the age of eight (many of these will be at school during the day except in the holidays)

They must also have at least half their staff trained to NVQ Level 3 (childcare and education). It follows that up to 50 per cent can be unqualified. There are plans to increase the proportion of qualified staff in the future but details were not announced in advance.

References

You would be wise to ask for references from parents who have used the services of the nursery which interests you. Take up at least two so that you can compare replies. Make your own checklist of questions to ask. For example:

● What did their children most enjoy about the nursery in question?

● Did they make friends?

● How relaxed were mealtimes?

● How much opportunity was there for outside play?

● How well planned were each day's activities?

● What did the children learn?

● Were the children happy?

● How often were the parents called in to take their children home early?

Which kind of nursery?

There are four main kinds of nursery:

● Local authority nurseries run by your local council – these are subsidised and have very strict entry qualifications.

● Community nurseries run for residents in your neighbourhood and mostly means-tested.

● Private nurseries run for profit.

● Workplace nurseries which are usually subsidised.

There are also nurseries which have an educational function – nursery classes (see separate entry).

Local authority nurseries

Local authority nurseries are, in theory, open to all. In practice, you are most likely to get a place if you are a lone parent or if you are on a low income. Working mothers on average incomes, especially those with partners to share their childcare, may not qualify for a place.

Most local authorities restrict places to those they consider to be 'in need'. They make up their own rules about what 'in need' means. In affluent areas, free places may be offered to mothers with relatively high incomes, provided they meet other criteria. You must be prepared to declare details of your income, welfare entitlements and family circumstances.

Many council nurseries provide excellent care and have better buildings and equipment than their local private equivalents. They tend to take larger numbers of children than private nurseries.

All local authority nurseries must comply with the rules of the Children Act in terms of staffing ratios and qualifications. But, unlike private nurseries, they do not have to be properly inspected.

Astonishing as it may seem, public nurseries run by local social services departments sometimes bypass fundamental safeguards. Private nurseries must register under the Children Act and be inspected by local social services departments every year. If they fail to meet the required standards, they can be closed down. But until now, council-run nurseries are not necessarily inspected in the same formal way because local authorities cannot inspect themselves.

This loophole in the law should be closed this year by the establishment of a new, national team of inspectors called the Early Years Directorate, under the control of the schools' inspectorate, OFSTED. They will have the right to regulate all childcare and education outside the home from the age of three months.

In the meantime, some councils try to keep their nurseries on their toes through a system of informal inspection, but if bad management practices start, they are very hard to stop. Unlike private nurseries, it is almost unknown for a local authority nursery to be closed down.

There have been several scandals involving children in public nurseries who have been left unsupervised. In one case, hidden cameras revealed a two-year-old choking on an object he had found in the playground, without the knowledge of the staff. Other children were seen playing unsupervised with scissors and other dangerous objects.

In another recent case in the North East of England, local authority nursery staff were found to have abused children by taking pornographic photographs of them. The staff were badly managed and their criminal behaviour went unchecked. Because of a loophole in the law, employees with criminal records are not necessarily subject to police checks.

'It's a nonsense,' said Lynn McCarthy, a childcare co-ordinator for the Leeds City Council Under Eights Service. 'In group care they are not considered to be as dangerous as someone working alone in a house. We can make sure workers in group care have a child protection check to see if they can spot the symptoms of abuse, we can make sure they have a health check to make sure they are fit, but we cannot enforce police checks. The police tell us they are not allowed to do it unless the nursery asks for it.'

Until proper independent inspection is brought in, parents must be vigilant. You can insist on correct staffing levels and correct numbers of qualified carers because these are relatively easy to count. You can, in the last resort, take the nursery to a civil court if it fails to come up to standard. Your local Citizens' Advice Bureau or Law Centre will advise you how to do this. But it will take a lot of time and effort. Prepare for at least a year's struggle.

Community nurseries
Community nurseries are semi-public forms of childcare. They are usually restricted to mothers who live nearby. This means you cannot normally choose one near your work. Many have long waiting lists. Like council nurseries, they are often subsidised. The money may come from the council itself, from central government, or from charities or religious groups. They are usually run by the staff and parents themselves through a management committee.

Unlike some council nurseries, they must be inspected by the local social services department every year. They also offer more places to children whose family income is average or above. Also, because they are self-governing, your voice will be heard if you notice things going wrong. The staff are more directly accountable.

As with a council nursery, you must be prepared to be means-tested. If you qualify, your name will go on the waiting list. Some community nurseries set aside places for full-cost customers, too. There is no general rule, you have to ask each community nursery in turn how much you have to pay. Usually, the fees are the equivalent of private nurseries in your area.

Private nurseries

Private nurseries are on the increase. The huge growth in their numbers is fuelled by the rising numbers of mothers who want to return to work. However, the more demand for their services, the more they cost.

The price can be as little as £90 for one child for a 50-hour week to as much as £200 per child. You have to compare the cost with that of local childminders and nannies to convince yourself that this is good value.

The cost of private nurseries puts them out of the reach of most lone mothers. However, that may have changed with the introduction of the new Working Families Tax Credit which began in late 1999. Those with savings of less than £8,000 may qualify for subsidies of up to 70 per cent to help pay for a nursery place or a childminder's services (see Chapter 5: Know Your Rights).

A few private nurseries take babies as young as six weeks old, but most have a starting age of two. The reason is the same as for public and community nurseries – cost. A nursery would find it hard to compete with a local childminder who can look after three babies in her own home without the expense of purpose-built premises. Most nurseries choose the easy option and refuse babies altogether.

There are encouraging signs, however. One nursery in Rawdon on the north-west fringes of Leeds has a dedicated baby room with a staff to child ratio of 1:2. It charges £20 a day for each child and is open from 7.30 in the morning until 7.30 at night. This is very good value, even though it costs more than many local mothers can afford. Whether a nursery near you can match such service depends on local property prices and labour costs. In expensive areas such as central London, the cost of renting premises large enough to have dedicated baby facilities could easily push the cost of a week's babycare to £200 per child or more.

A new accreditation scheme for nurseries was launched in May 2000 by the National Day Nurseries Association. This is intended to award quality assurance certificates to all nurseries which meet the organisation's highest standards. You can check which local nurseries qualify by calling NDNA on 01484 541641.

Workplace nurseries (creches)

There are far too few workplace nurseries in this country. A government survey carried out in 1996 showed only one in ten employers provided any practical help with childcare. Most of the ones which did were in the private sector in organisations with large numbers of young women workers. Of the 28 per cent of mothers who chose not to return to work, most said the reason was a lack of adequate childcare, especially the absence of workplace nurseries or an allowance to help pay for other kinds of childcare. There are only 600 workplace nurseries in the entire United Kingdom. They are subsidised and open to employees of the organisation which pays. However, some employers prefer to offer mothers childcare vouchers which can be used for a childminder, a nanny or a nursery near their home. Others provide nothing.

Penny Hughes, the former president of Coca Cola UK, rejected workplace creches for her employees when she was in charge.

'It is forcing people to bring their child to work and saying it is right to put them there,' she said. 'We preferred to fund places in a locally-run day care nursery which enabled people to make the choice. We did not want to have children coming into the same building. I think that's quite difficult. It distracts. I've seen some creches in the States where you can flick on a switch and go through a video network and look in and see how your child is. I think that is interfering with the working day.'

The advantage of a creche is that it is near your workplace if there is an emergency. Also, like private nurseries, most creches must be inspected by the local authority to make sure they are safe. Unlike a nanny, therefore, the standard of care is monitored.

The disadvantage is that they can turn you into a doting mother, visiting your child during breaks, worrying about them if they have had a bad morning, neglecting your work.

Another obvious disadvantage is that a workplace nursery goes with the job. If you are fired or leave your job, your child will be expelled from the creche at the same time. This can be traumatic. The relationships he or she has built up with the staff and the other children will be instantly severed.

If you choose a nursery near your work, on the other hand, you will have some leeway, and your child will have the opportunity to say a longer goodbye. Choose a nursery near your home, and he or she can stay there until you find another job.

Some workplace nurseries, like those in hospitals for National Health Service workers, are exempt for registration under the Children Act because they are on Crown property. They are not legally required to be inspected every year. To find out if your workplace nursery falls into this category ask the manager how often inspections take place.

Ask who carries them out. Satisfy yourself that staffing levels are up to standard and at least half the staff have NVQ Level 3 certificates. There may be nothing to worry about, but it is best to make sure.

The baby who went to hospital every day: *Melanie was lucky in her choice of nursery when her first child, David, was born. Her husband worked as a doctor at a local hospital. The hospital had a staff nursery and would take babies as young as six months.*

She said: 'As soon as I was pregnant I booked my place. I was just about to start work as a management trainee with Unilever. I started the baby off as early as he could go which was six months old and I would take him one day a week. I gently ramped it up to three days a week which was when I started part-time work. Then I went full-time and the baby went to the nursery full-time as well.'

'It was a very large nursery with quite a lot of flexibility because they had a bit of extra capacity in their system. They catered for nurses starting at a quarter past seven for their early shifts. It was a very large and institutionalised environment for young children and some mothers would not want it for their children. Some prefer the family environment of a childminder or a nanny but I was happy with the standard of childcare it offered.'

Because a workplace nursery is either on or near your work premises, it is relatively easy to ask the other mothers for information.

- How much did their children enjoy it?
- Were the facilities as good as those in nearby nurseries?
- How well were the day's activities planned?
- How appropriate were the activities to their child's ages and abilities?
- How much learning went on?
- How much were the children involved in planning the day's play?
- What were the agreed punishments and rewards?
- What happened if your child fell ill?
- How much flexibility was there if you were asked to work late?
- What was the standard of the food given to the children?
- What information were you given by the staff about your child's day?

It may not be polite to look a gift-horse in the mouth, but you must know your child is being well cared for, even if your boss is paying.

The student doctor who used sports club and supermarket creches:
Single mother Dreena from Glasgow joined a sports club creche when she was studying to become a doctor. She also took her baby to Safeway's supermarket so that she could use its creche, too. Dreena became pregnant in her early thirties while she was a nurse. The child's father, a Frenchman, gave her no financial support.

'I could not afford private childminders,' she said. 'The biggest hurdle was the cost of childcare. Christopher's father wanted nothing to do with the pregnancy. I owe an enormous amount to friends who helped by taking Christopher for odd evenings or weekends.'

'I used to take him to Safeway's supermarket creche on Saturday and Sunday mornings so I could sit and study in the cafe. I joined a sports club so I could use their creche and revise in their canteen.'

Six years after she started studying, Dreena qualified as a doctor and now works at Glasgow's Southern General Hospital. She is still critical of childcare provision, especially by employers.

'Employers need to open their eyes more to the needs of single parents. Few provide creches and those that do don't provide them to match the hours many people work. Companies need to ask what women can offer them and work it out from there. Employers are losing out by not doing that because women have a lot to offer.'

6. Nursery classes

Nursery classes are usually attached to a school. The idea is to provide early learning for children aged three to five, with a range of structured educational experiences which develop and stimulate their minds. They have been dubbed the 'fast track' to primary school.

This is a departure from the idea that children in the two years before school should simply socialise and play. There is still some debate about whether formal learning is a good thing for children of such tender years. However, the current wisdom is to regard early education and day care as two sides of the same coin, with nurseries and even childminders encouraged to accept nursery education grants.

Advantages and disadvantages
The big advantage of nursery classes is that they often guarantee your child a place in the primary school of your choice. In well-run classes, your child will be supervised by as many adults as in a nursery and get extra educational stimulus as well.

By comparison with nurseries, however, nursery classes are often inconvenient. They usually close at the end of the school day which means you either have to take time off work to pick them up in the middle of the afternoon or employ someone like a mother's help or an au pair to do it for you. They work best if you have an older child at the school who needs collecting anyway.

Inspection and regulation
There are hidden dangers in nursery classes. Council social services inspectors have no right of entry unless they are registered under the Children Act. In local authority schools, this may be of small concern since welfare issues are to some extent subject to council scrutiny. However, private schools fall outside councils' remit altogether because nursery classes are inspected by OFSTED, the schools' inspectorate, rather than the social services departments of local councils.

OFSTED inspectors are concerned with standards of education not with child welfare issues. They have no powers to enforce the stringent staffing levels of nurseries. Some private schools, for example, are reportedly overcrowding their nursery classes to earn more money. One recently documented case involved a nursery class with 15 children aged between two-and-a-half and five, supervised by one adult. Had it been a nursery, as many as four adults would have been required. According to the National Day Nurseries Association, three-year-olds are sometimes taught in classes with pupil–teacher ratios of up to 1:40.

'Local authorities are extremely annoyed,' said Rosemary Murphy, the chief executive of the National Day Nurseries Association, a charity which represents thousands of nurseries through Britain. 'They are champing at the bit because they can't get into them to inspect.

'The law is an ass. It's a massive loophole. Private schools are inspected every four to five years, but the inspectors are not the same as the ones who regulate nurseries. They are experts on the education of school-age children. They are not really equipped to look at the care and education of children up to five.'

The government has plans to unify the inspection of schools and nurseries under a body called the Early Years Directorate. It may also change the law to bring nursery classes in line with standards applied to nurseries. But this is likely to take more than a year.

In the meantime, if you like the idea of nursery education for your child, you should look for nursery classes with staffing levels the equivalent of those in nurseries – one adult to eight pupils aged between three and eight, one adult to every four pupils aged two to three.

7. Pre-Schools – the playgroup network

There are around 17,500 'pre-school' groups in Britain (formerly known as playgroups), though their numbers are declining largely through competition with pre-school classes attached to primary schools. When nursery vouchers were introduced briefly in 1996–1998, schools scrambled to attract four-year-olds whose parents had vouchers worth £1,100 a year to spend on nursery and reception classes. But because the pupil–teacher ratios for schools were less stringent than for playgroups, some four-year-olds found themselves in classes of 40 children or more. Childcare ratios in pre-school playgroups are mostly much better than nursery classes or nursery schools. Those accredited by the Pre-School Learning Alliance under a new quality assurance scheme have ratios of one adult to every six children. The maximum ratio for the organisation's pre-schools is 1:8. Most voluntary-sector pre-school groups offer childcare for three to five-year-olds for only half the day. This may be enough to enable you to work part-time.

A few also offer training for adults. There are about 40,000 adults on courses attached to pre-schools every year. This is particularly valuable for anyone who would like to learn a new skill such as computing or driving. In Leicester, for example, unemployed parents can join a car mechanics' course while their children are cared for in a creche. After eight weeks, they take an examination. If they pass, they are given free driving lessons and a free driving test which may help them find work.

8. Family and friends – the traditional solution

The extended family is alive and well – if a little fragmented. The days when grandparents, parents, aunts, uncles, brothers and sisters all lived within walking distance of each other are long gone. However, family members are still the most commonly-used childcarers in the country.

Money is usually the most important factor in choosing relatives as childcarers. This is not surprising when you consider how much income most mothers lose when they return to work. The Centre for Analysis of Social Exclusion found in 1999 that women in Britain experience a much greater drop in wages when they have children than other industrialised countries such as the US, Canada and Sweden.

Even among full-time workers, women with children in Britain get less than childless colleagues. They lose about eight per cent of income when they have their first child, and over thirty per cent when they have three or more children. In my experience, some mothers lose this much after one child. In Sweden, mothers' pay stays the same no matter how many children they have.

Childminders often charge £125 a week or more for 50 hours' care of one child. You would have to earn at least £250 after tax to make employing a childminder worthwhile – unless your job is so important to you that you are prepared to spend all your income on childcare and travelling to and from work. Also, with a childminder or a nanny, you are dealing with strangers – until you have built up a relationship of trust. You know your family already. You know whether or not you can trust them to look after your child to the same standards that you would apply yourself.

The mother who chose grandparents for full-time childcare: *'I didn't want a stranger getting involved with my child on a personal level, standing in as a mother figure,' says Catherine from Leeds, whose three-year-old daugher Bethany is cared for by both sets of grandparents in turn, while she works full-time as a microbiologist. She rejected childminders even though her company offered hefty subsidies.*

'I was worried with a childminder that she might see her as more of a mother figure than me. I don't mind that with the grandmas at all, the closer they are the better. Also the grandparents will bring your child up the same way you were brought up with the same values and the same sort of discipline.'

Catherine's choice of grandparents as childcarers came after her sister found looking after Bethany too difficult. She was considering nurseries when both her mother and her partner's mother stepped in. One lives nearby and looks after Bethany for three days. The other looks after Bethany for two days. It involves Catherine in long journeys. She travels eight miles to Morley on the south side of Leeds, a trip which means leaving home at seven o'clock to be at work for eight-fifteen.

Research by the charity Age Concern shows that one grandparent in four cares for children while parents go out to work. In many families, the mothers would not be able to work without this support, which is often unpaid. Where grandparents look after the children, they usually do so for around three hours a week. However, one million grandparents in Britain do so for more than 15 hours.

These days, grandparent care is rarely under one family roof. Parents often travel long distances every day to grandparents or other relatives, leave their children in the morning and pick them up after work.

There is also increasing evidence that grandparents are taking a smaller role in the care of their grandchildren than they did twenty years ago. Geoff Dench, a senior research fellow at the Institute of Community Studies and a professor of sociology at the University of Middlesex, has interviewed more than 2,500 grandparents around Britain and found that four in ten said they wanted a life more free from family duties.

The reasons are often practical. Most grandparents are still workers when their grandchildren are very young. Why should they lose substantial income by giving up their jobs to look after their children's children? Those who have retired have the time to do the job, but may not be physically strong enough to cope with a boisterous two-year-old for more than the occasional afternoon.

The evidence also suggests that grandparents do not want to be childminders. Many are in conflict about the way their grandchildren are brought up. They often see them as spoiled brats whose parents have failed to instill proper discipline. They would rather the parents got on with the primary childcare in their own way than be forced to take on the role of stern guardians of family standards. That way, they can earn the love of their grandchildren without having the irksome responsibility of deciding how they should be brought up.

The seventy-mile round trip: *Medical secretary Fiona from Kilbirnie in Ayrshire and her husband Paul have longer journeys than most parents taking their children for childcare. She and Paul get up at 6 o'clock every morning. They get their 18-month-old daughter Neave dressed and fed and set off for work at 7am. Paul drops Fiona off at her workplace in Paisley 20 miles away. She starts work at 7.45am and finishes at 5.15pm. Paul then drives Neave to her grandparents' house in Renfrew and leaves her there while he drives another 10 miles to East Kilbride to the south of Glasgow, where he has a job as a social worker looking after clients with learning difficulties.*

'We both decided to work four days a week,' says Paul. 'That way, we can spend more time with Neave. I find it hard leaving her after weekends because we've both built up our relationship with her again.'

Two days every fortnight, Paul's mother, who is retired, drives to their house to look after Neave. She suffers from M.E. and finds it hard to cope. Fiona and Paul have decided to move house to be nearer her parents. Their new house will cost far more than the one they are selling but they plan travel to work by bus, thus saving the money they were spending on their car.

Paul is aware that the grandparents have different ideas about Neave's upbringing from his own. 'They teach her a lot of stuff that I wouldn't teach her. We have different points of view. What we say to Neave at weekends sort of peels away during the week.'

The disadvantages of relatives as childcarers

Here is the rub. With family, you do not have as much say as with professional childcarers. If your child's grandmother believes in smacking and you do not, how are you going to make sure she does things your way? If your sister thinks it is all right for your child to watch TV all day, how are you going to persuade her otherwise? If grandpa smokes heavily in the same room as your baby, how can you make him stop?

By contrast, when you pay someone to look after your children, whether it is a childminder, a nanny or the manager of a nursery, that person has to satisfy you. If she fails, her reputation is on the line. With professional childcare, you have to be choosy. You pick someone who is on your wavelength. With your own family, you have to take what you get.

'I often get mothers who have their child looked after by granny but aren't happy about it,' says Lynn McCarthy, the childcare co-ordinator for Elida Fabergé in Leeds. 'They ask me how they can tell their own parent that they do not want them to continue to look after their child.

'If it is to do with the standard of childcare, I usually say they should wait until there's a natural break in the child's life, such as when they first go to pre-school playgroup. Then they can switch to a childminder or whichever other form of childcare they prefer. If it's a relationship problem with granny, I can't really help. They must work it out for themselves.'

This conflict is often worse when the grandparent is not the mother's parent. The customs of your partner's family may conflict with those of your own upbringing. If this difference of approach is unacceptable but you do not wish to cause offence, use any change of circumstance, such as an alteration of your working hours (which you bring about), as an excuse to change your childcare arrangements.

An alternative is to bring granny's childcare skills up to scratch by asking her to register as a childminder. That way, her home will be brought up to standard and she will have to undergo training in proper methods of childcare. There is strong backing for this idea from government circles. The problem comes if granny then slips back into her old habits. What are you going to do? Have her struck off?

Partners as joint carers

You could, of course, enlist your partner's help with childcare. Unlike other relatives, you have chosen your partner. You are likely to have similar ideas about how you want your children to be looked after. This is why more and more couples are beginning to find ways of adjusting both their jobs to allow them to share childcare between them.

The father who gave up his well-paid job: *James Dean decided to give up his job as an Institutional Equity salesman in the City of London to become a full-time carer to his three children, Imogen (seven), Oliver (five) and Adam (one). His wife, Angela, continued to work as a managing director of a global investment bank. James did not intend to take on the role full-time, but his children preferred their father to nannies.*

'They say: "We like our new nanny, he's daddy" which used to irritate me,' said James. 'But I've become used to it. I started because I wasn't enjoying my job. I did not see a lot of future in it and Angela was earning ten times more than I was. We realised that we did not both need to work and that it would be better for the family if one of us was giving more time.

'We had had a few bad experiences with nannies. One was rather hard on the children. She had a significant temper and we got feedback from the children about they way she treated them. Besides it made more sense for me to help them with their homework than someone whose education was not very advanced. I don't feel I've lost status, though my mother is disappointed. She paid for my education and pushed me and my brother through Oxford. She keeps asking me if I've got a job yet. My father-in-law can be worse, especially when he hears that I've just turned a job down. It's the general middle-England expectation that it's the man who goes out and fends.

'Angela hopes to stop in two or three years' time and I'll find a job to maintain a family interest in the work culture... we might swap roles.

For the moment, the children are far less resentful because I'm looking after them. Angela sets off for work at six in the morning before they get up and is often not back until eight. But she's home most weekends. The children have coped well. Their response has been one of the main causes of our change of mindset.'

Not every partner can cope as well as this. It helped that James lived in an inner-city street where people minded their own business and accepted their neighbours for what they were. He was under no pressure to conform to local people's conventions about how fathers should behave. This would have been far more difficult in a village or small town where everyone might have known him and would have asked him if he had 'got a job yet'.

Some fathers feel a real sense of loss if they give up paid work to look after their children. Jenny's husband, Peter, was a case in point.

The father who could not cope as a househusband: Peter had lost his job. Jenny suggested that he should look after their children. Without his regular income, they could not afford professional childcare in the inner city. But the change was traumatic for Peter.

Within months, the stress of having no job and trying to do everything for his young children had exhausted him to the point of breakdown. Jenny had to give up her job instantly. The family moved to a cheaper home in the country to give them a little cash to live on while they sorted themselves out. She then reinvented herself as a freelance writer and was able to play a much greater part in the raising of her children. Her husband retrained for a new career and the family managed to stay intact.

'It was touch and go,' said Jenny. 'Luckily our children were quite young when the crisis hit us. Maddy was five and Josh was three. I couldn't have guessed that Peter would become so stressed so quickly. I don't think he had realised how much he had identified with his job. I hadn't realised how difficult it would be for him to look after the children. He had coped really well when he had a job and did his fair share of childcare, but to do it all the time was very different. He felt trapped.'

Most partners do not attempt to change roles so dramatically. They adjust their work patterns to fit in with childcare. This, in many respects, is becoming the new ideal, the way many of us would like to organise our family lives. But it is a much more complex affair than the traditional family. To make it work, both parents have to make compromises, juggle timetables, sacrifice free time.

The early-bird father: *Jeff is typical of the new breed of father. Brought up in a traditional family in Liverpool, in which his father had almost nothing to do with childcare, Jeff takes his two-year-old daughter Sam to nursery or grandparents every day, a round trip of around 40 miles. He and his wife, Jill, live in Warrington. She works in the stock department of a shop in Warrington , he is a printing technician in Liverpool.*

'We all get up at about 6.15, wash, shower and change, get the baby ready, drop Jill off, the baby and I come back home and have a bit of breakfast. She works seven till twelve. Two days Sam goes to the nursery in Liverpool which is paid for by my firm, and the other three are split between my mum and dad and Jill's mum and dad. I work 8.30 to 4.45 in Liverpool. On Tuesdays and Wednesdays, Jill's mum and dad come over to our place from Runcorn and Jill looks after Sam in the afternoons when she's finished work.

Sam's two now and I've been off work three or four times with her when she's been ill. I love looking after her. My own dad wasn't that involved with us when we were kids. But we didn't have Sam lightly, she wasn't a mistake. When Jill was pregnant we were over the moon and I had no intention of being a passenger. I couldn't personally see how you could do it any different.'

Friends as joint carers

Friends can also share your childcare with you. If you know someone with young children whom you like and trust, you may be able to work out joint childcare arrangements. This does not necessarily mean leaving your child at her house all day in the manner of a childminder. It is more likely to involve care for part of the day, such as allowing your friend to collect your child from a nursery alongside her own and looking after him or her until you come home from work.

The child-share: *Melanie from Doncaster has a part-time job as a clerical worker in a local engineering company. She has two children, Ben aged three and 18-month-old Natalie. Her friend Debbie, used to live next door. She has a daughter, Sarah, aged three.*

'Having two kids the same age was great. We used to be in and out of each others' houses all day,' said Melanie. 'Then Debbie split up from her

partner and had to move house. But we kept in touch and a few months after Natalie was born, Debbie had this offer of some part-time work at a call centre and asked me if I could look after Sara part of the day. I said I could if she did opposite shifts to me. I was on maternity leave at the time. I went to my boss and asked if I could go back part-time. He agreed if I could work mornings.

'It works really well. Debbie comes over with Sarah to my house every morning about half past seven and we get the kids' breakfast together. I work eight-thirty to twelve-thirty and her shift starts at two o' clock. Luckily I can walk to work so I'm back home by a quarter to one to take over with the kids until half past six. I think it works because we knew each other so well before and the kids get on great. It's better for Ben to have someone to play with. Occasionally my mum will take over in the afternoons if I want to go to the shops or I have to take Natalie to the hospital.'

Single parents often depend on friends more than mothers with partners. With young children, it can make good sense to work out a child-sharing arrangement with a friend who has children of the same age, rather than impose on unwilling grandparents. With older children it is more difficult, especially when the older child is adopted.

The adoptive mother who depends on friends and family: *Lynne is a social worker in Greater Manchester. She is single and depends on her friends a great deal to help look after the daughter she adopted three years ago. Simone was eight when the adoption went through. Lynne had to give up her job managing a daycentre because her employers found it too difficult to let her go part-time. She had to find another career at her time of greatest stress.*

'My friends were my lifeline,' she said. 'I needed someone to share my thoughts with because dealing with an eight-year-old who has been through some very bad times is extremely emotionally exhausting. You've not only got a relationship with an eight-year-old to cope with, but you've got to make up for the eight years you didn't have with them. There's a lot of additional parenting you've got to do. Being single, I relied on my family and friends for support. Luckily, they all live fairly close by. They would babysit for me and occasionally they took her overnight. It meant I could have a night off occasionally. It also meant Simone could stay with other children her own age.'

If you know someone at work who also has a baby, you might even suggest some kind of childcare-sharing arrangement in which you take turns to work and look after each other's children. You need a lot of trust to make it work effectively, particularly if you depend on each other to be on time for a daily handover. Some mothers manage to work five days every fortnight, three days one week and two the next, alternating their shift patterns with the other mother in the childshare. In the next chapter, Work Options, you can find out about the range of choices some employers now offer.

9. Out-of-school childcare

The huge increase in the numbers of working mothers has finally brought a response from local authority education departments. The number of homework clubs and breakfast clubs run by schools, employers, charities and other organisations has grown dramatically in recent years in recognition of the inconvenience of normal school hours and the need for children to have structured play or supervision both before formal lessons begin and after they finish.

Some, like the Littlewoods Little Rascals Club in Manchester, are run for the benefit of company employees. The club opens at seven in the morning until nine to allow mothers (and fathers) to drop their children off before they start work. It re-opens at 3.30 to take in employees' children who have finished school and look after them until their parents are ready to pick them up. This is effectively nursery care with a little homework supervision thrown in.

In the village of Bottesford in Leicestershire, the local Women's Institute runs an after-school club with toys and games. The group does not have the resources to supervise homework. Again, it is a kind of nursery care.

Others, like those run by schools themselves, are more academically inclined. Many schools now see homework clubs as a way of boosting their results by extending the school day. Some raise funds for this purpose.

Information about before- and after-school clubs is patchy because there is no centralised organisation in charge. You must do your own homework to find out if the school of your choice offers any facilities and what level of staff to pupils is available. If it does not, you must ask other parents if their children attend similar schemes run by voluntary organisations or companies.

Pupil–teacher ratios are not laid down by law and you have to satisfy yourself that supervision is adequate. Even though your children may be older, you should still ask the kinds of questions you might put to a nursery.

10. Holiday play projects

Only three per cent of employers run holiday playschemes. The rules which apply to nurseries do not apply to holiday play clubs. You should therefore run through a checklist similar to the one you might use for a nursery to satisfy yourself that your child will be safe. You need to know:

- the staff to child ratio (1:8 is good if the children are over three years old)
- the qualifications of the staff, including first-aid and teaching certificates
- the timetable of activities planned (with opt-outs for your child if you feel there is a risk)
- the standard of accommodation provided on residential projects and the supervision of the children at night
- emergency arrangements if your child is ill.

There is no centralised register of holiday play schemes because they are run by such a large number of disparate organisations. Some are local authority controlled and must therefore comply with the staff–pupil ratios of nurseries. Others, like computer camps or company play schemes, are rarely if ever inspected. You have to rely on your own judgement as to whether or not your child is safe.

Childcare Checklist – at a glance

To recap, there are ten childcare options:

1. Childminders. Budget 'sole-charge' childcare in a home setting. No compulsory formal training, but all must be registered with the local authority and vetted by the police. Their premises must be inspected annually. Childminders are limited to three children under the age of five and another three aged five to eight. Cost is between £1.50 and £4 an hour, (£75–£200 per 50-hour week) depending on location.

2. Nannies. Flexible childcare in your own home, suitable for 'sole charge' of children of all ages. Costly unless you share with another mother. No compulsory training, but many train to NVQ Level 3 in childcare and education. Unregulated – no national or local register and no option for vetting by the police – parents must make their own checks. Nanny agencies voluntary 'quality assurance' scheme to be introduced. No limit on numbers of children. Cost is £150–£350 per 45-hour week depending on area and the nanny's experience and qualifications. Live-out nannies cost more than those who live in.

3. Mother's Helps. Housekeepers who help with the household chores and assist you in looking after your children. No regulation. No option for police vetting. Ideal for mothers who work from home, but not suitable for 'sole-charge' of children. Most live out and work part-time in your home. Cost is £4–£6 an hour (£150–£240 per 45-hour week) depending on location and duties.

4. Au pairs. Useful temporary foster daughters, who can help out with childcare for little cost, but must never be left in sole charge especially of pre-school children. No option for vetting by police. Usually young students of English from other countries. If from outside the EC can stay no more than two years. Maximum 30-hour week. Cost is around £40 a week plus board and lodging.

5. Nurseries. Relatively inflexible hours, no one-to-one childcare, but more playmates and better play facilities. Best for mothers with regular nine-to-five jobs and one or two children aged two to five. Expensive for mothers with large families. No problems with staff holidays or illness, unlike personal carers. Can be inflexible if your child is ill or you are late for pickup. Subject to police vetting and annual inspections though a few loopholes in the law remain. All nurseries subject to strict rules about staff numbers. Cost varies from £90–£200 per child for 50-hour week.

6. Nursery classes. Usually attached to schools to provide early learning as well as play for children aged two to five. Not adequately inspected or regulated until new Early Years Directorate takes control. No limits on class sizes supervised by one adult. Best practice is to mimic nursery-style standards of staffing – one adult to every four pupils aged two to three, one adult to every eight pupils aged three to five. Most open during school hours only. Best for mothers with another child at same school. Cost usually between £70 and £150 per child for 35-hour week.

7. Pre-schools. Usually half-day care for children aged three to five in nurseries run by voluntary groups. Subject to same regulations and inspections as nurseries. Staff vetted by police. Quality assurance scheme run by Pre-School Learning Alliance to give ratios of one adult to every six children. Cost usually between £40 and £100 for a 20-hour week.

8. Family and friends. The no-cost option (providing they are close by) with flexibility and one-to-one care built in. No regulation of standards. Conflicts over discipline styles commonplace. Some grandparents may not be physically or mentally capable of 'sole charge'. Grandparents' home may have hidden dangers for young children. Government encouraging grandparents to register as childminders to raise standards of care. Friends who swap childcare must co-ordinate handovers reliably.

9. Out-of-school clubs. Temporary nursery care before and after school, often from 7–9am and from 3.30–5.30pm. Subject to same inspections and police vetting as nurseries though some loopholes remain. Cost usually £40–£60 for 20-hour week.

10. Holiday play projects. Each scheme is unique. Some offer full nursery care for children aged two to fifteen on a first come, first served basis. Others limit by age or numbers. Subject to same inspections and police vetting as nurseries though some loopholes remain. Cost £50–£200 per 50-hour week.

Organising backup

So far, so organised. But you must also plan your backup arrangements. What if your baby catches flu and cannot go to the nursery or the childminder for fear of passing the virus on? What if you are forced to work late and you cannot pick your baby up at the appointed hour?

You need to find out who might be able to cover for you in such a crisis before it actually happens. Often this will be a friend or neighbour and it might be wise to work out a reward for their help before you need to call on their services. You can offer to pay them an hourly rate so that they do not feel exploited if your 'hour's delay' turns into two hours. You may never need your fall-back arrangements, but they will reduce the amount of stress and guilt.

Even if you can afford a live-in nanny, there is no excuse for assuming that you can telephone at a moment's notice and expect her to work late merely because she has a room in your house. She must be able to count on finishing on time so that she can meet her friends or go to a concert or whatever else she plans for the evenings.

I was a prime candidate for bad time-keeping. I worked in newspapers and my husband was an independent radio producer. Both jobs often required us to work late from time to time. We decided to draw up a contract for our nanny's basic working week, which included one evening of babysitting per week. The day we chose varied from week to week. We would give at least one day's notice and we would pay overtime for any extra hours worked. It was all spelled out clearly and fairly.

This made the problem go away. It is rare than any of us has less than a day's warning of late working. In my case, the nanny always had twenty-four hours to cancel any arrangements she had made or arrange a substitute baby-sitter. She soon had a network of substitutes organised, just in case. There is no reason why similar arrangements could not be made with a childminder, a mother's help or an au pair – provided you do not abuse your privileges.

Genuine emergencies are a different matter. You cannot give twenty-four hours notice of being involved in a car accident, for example. All you can do is give as much warning as possible. A call at 3pm warning that you are likely to be two hours later than your normal 6pm homecoming at least gives your childcarer the chance to put your fall-back arrangements into motion.

4: WORK OPTIONS

Not so very long ago, there used to be no such thing as flexible working. Family life and work were put into two separate compartments. Women who became pregnant had to give up work and stay at home to look after the children until they were all at school. Fathers carried on working as if their families did not exist. Working hours were arranged to suit the employer not the employee. It seemed to be the natural order of things.

The collapse of traditional manufacturing and extraction industries changed all that. Millions of men's jobs disappeared. New service industries sprang up offering jobs more suited to women's skills than men's.

At first, employers made no concessions to family life. Working mothers worked standard hours. Flexible working practices were almost unheard of. Nursery provision was almost non-existent. If a mother wanted time to pick up her children from school, she had to give up full-time employment and take a part-time job, which was almost always badly paid.

There was condemnation of mothers who worked. They, not their employers, were responsible for neglecting their children. The phrase 'latchkey kids' was coined to describe the children who arrived home an hour before their mothers and had to look after themselves until they returned home. In effect, mothers were made to feel guilty for working the shift patterns their employers had imposed on them.

Only now is a new model of family life emerging, one that is built around the notion of parents working and looking after their families at the same time. This involves not only recasting the image of mothers, but of fathers, too. It means radically rethinking the notion of the working day. There is still resistance to change. Employers must be presented with a strong business case for being flexible.

Later in this chapter, mothers who have succeeded will discuss the strategies they employed. There will also be a framework for you to plan your own strategies and develop arguments which are likely to appeal to your boss.

Employer of the Year

It helps, of course, if you can give examples of other firms which have allowed flexible working, such as Littlewoods, the stores and football pools group based in Liverpool and Manchester which won the 1999 Employer of the Year award organised by the charity Parents at Work with Lloyds TSB bank.

It offers its 27,000 workers a choice of 160 different shift patterns to help them fit in the care of children or the elderly. They can work part time, during school hours, during school term times, they can job-share and they can work from home.

In addition, there are nursery facilities and a holiday play scheme at the firm's Liverpool headquarters. In Manchester, it offers a pre-school club and an after-school club for the children of workers. All full-time employees are allowed five days' paid leave a year for 'unplanned domestic activities' such as when a nursery calls to say their child is ill and needs to be taken home.

Even ten years ago, this might all have seemed a waste of money, an extra expense which cut into profits. But Littlewoods say it is good for business as well as being caring.

'We have noticed a much greater loyalty and commitment to the firm,' says Surinder Sharma, the firm's corporate Equal Opportunities Manager. 'When mothers take maternity leave, 98 per cent of them come back. This means we do not have the expense of recruiting new employees and training them. We have reduced absenteeism and our productivity has risen, because mothers aren't worrying about the care of their children or elderly relatives. They can concentrate on their jobs.'

There are other benefits to the firm. When there are production emergencies, employees are prepared to come in early or work late, knowing they will be given time off later if they need it. Surveys have shown that Littlewoods' customers are happier, too, because they are better treated by Littlewoods' employees than those of rival firms. Their delivery business has expanded and now includes retailers such as Tesco, Safeway and Harrods.

Littlewoods also feels it is on the winning side of the ethical war in the clothing trade. It supplies clothes for five outlets including Hawkshead, Racing Green and Principles. In the long term, it hopes customers will prefer garments made by workers who are well-treated.

'Issues like child labour are getting through to customers,' says Surinder Sharma. 'If you have three different brands of shirt of the same quality and price, you will choose the label made by the company whose values you agree with.'

Well over half the workers at Littlewoods work flexible hours and of these about a quarter are men. Few men, however, opt for part-time work, preferring to alter their hours to help with childcare rather than reduce them. The firm is encouraging men to take more options such as part-time working so that their partners can also return to work while they look after the children. It is a radical policy. Yet it is still comparatively new. Before the mid-1980s, attitudes weren't so accommodating.

Before and after flexible working policies: Norma Fleming worked for Littlewoods in Liverpool as a computer programmer before the great culture change. She remembers it well.

'When I had my son Robert in 1982, I came back to work full time because part-time work wasn't on offer. I don't think anyone was sufficiently interested to push for it,' she said. 'But when I had my daughter in 1986, the offer of part-time work had become available. One of the senior managers was far-sighted enough to realise that he was losing valuable staff. He thought it was worth having someone three days a week rather than losing all those skills.

'To have replaced me in a job as specialised as this, to bring somebody in brand new is a very expensive thing to have to do, it's not just the training cost it's the experience as well. It's very much a two-way thing, it's not just out of the goodness of their heart, I think both parties have something to gain from it.

'I came back to work three days a week after Amy was born. I worked Monday, Tuesday and Wednesday. It meant I had the contact of going out to work and keeping my hand in career-wise, but I still had four days at home. It always felt like you were at home more than you were at work. It didn't feel like work took over your life.'

When Norma's daughter was seven, she began to work four days a week. Three years later, her marriage broke up and she needed extra income. She asked if she could work full time. Her boss agreed immediately.

'It came at a very good time because my son was almost 15 and old enough to be left to his own devices to a very large degree, but my daughter was only ten and I had to look after her during the summer holidays. Then,

coincidentally, Littlewoods started up a play scheme in a school near to work in central Liverpool.

'Without the play scheme I would have had to pay out a lot of money to care for her or take huge amounts of holiday doing childcare myself. That would have meant we would have had very little time to spend on a family holiday.'

Following suit

Littlewoods is not an exceptional case. It is a mainstream company, a bigger version of thousands of similar ventures throughout the UK. It has its own high street stores such as Littlewoods and Index. It is in the financial services industry in a joint venture with the Woolwich. It has a television venture with Granada. Its home delivery service, Business Express, delivers goods for Tesco, Safeway and Harrods. It runs the Littlewoods Pools football competitions. It supplies clothes for many big-name high street stores and catalogue companies such as Principles, Dorothy Perkins, Racing Green and Hawkshead.

The trouble is that very few employers, especially in small companies, believe that the Littlewoods experience has anything to do with their business. They are deeply suspicious that family-friendly policies will lose them money. They regard it as a kind of welfare: the employee gains and the company loses. It is of little value citing cases where both sides gain such as the Buckinghamshire business information company which has structured its entire business around the school holidays so that working parents can take time off. Such examples are merely regarded as one-offs – freakish, not invented here and not applicable here.

This is why you have to make out a business case for flexible working without asking your employer to change everything overnight. Joy McMillan, the director of the Grow Trust, which campaigns for more flexible working for parents of both sexes, said:

'We suggest that you negotiate with your employers by arguing the business merits of part-time working. You should not do so as a mother or father returning to work after the birth of a baby asking for a favour. You should argue that your skills are still needed and that you have worked out an arrangement that will benefit both sides.'

A typical reaction to anyone asking for flexible working hours is likely to be that your job is not suited to it. In a recent BBC documentary about working mothers, senior manager Penny Tyler was told she could not alter her hours, even though she did not want to work less. Her boss Steve Oxley of Candlelight Products in Sheffield said: 'On the production side of the business where someone is in a senior position managing or supervising, you can't have them working different hours to the people they're looking after. Where problems arise, they need to be tackled straight away.'

This is nonsense. Countless other employers have discovered that a combination of delegation and mobile telephones can allow much more flexibility. Managers and supervisors need deputies to cover for periods of holiday or illness. Those same deputies can accommodate flexible working, too. Sue Chamberlain, the general manager of two department stores in Walsall, puts this into practice every day.

'If I'm a manager who can't afford to be out of the store then I'm not doing my job right. I run two units, I can't be in two places at once. I've got a duty manager in my other unit. You have to develop your people to be able to run the business without you. In my first promotion to a supervisor many years ago I was told the success would show when you could actually leave the business and the business would run as well if not better than when you were there.'

The best way to make out a business case for flexible working is to arm yourself with information about how schemes such as job-sharing, special leave and flexitime operate elsewhere, then try to apply each solution to your own circumstances. You must also assess the value of your own skills to your employer and allow the most important of these to be retained. If, for example, you have dual roles as an organiser and a contributor, it may be the first that is the more valuable. Your employer may be dreading the notion of training up someone new and untested. Play on that. Emphasise the cost that might be involved, not only in recruiting a replacement, but in taking time out for supervision.

It is always a good idea to have more than one option in mind when you present your case for flexible working. Here are ten to choose from.

Flexible working options

1. Part-time working

Part-time working usually means keeping your job but working far fewer hours, often only half your previous workload. It can also mean switching jobs to something less demanding or finding a new job which is only available for part of the day.

According to recent government statistics (Social Focus on Women and Men 1998), three quarters of working mothers return to work by the time their baby is eleven months old. Almost half work part time, often in low-paid jobs. Another quarter go back full time. They tend to be older, earn more and can afford full-time childcare.

Many of these full-time workers would like to reduce their hours to spend more time with their children – if their employers would let them. However, their companies do not want the expense of recruiting someone else to fill in the hours a working mother wants to set aside for childcare. Even if someone within the organisation can take over, it means re-organising several people's jobs to make it all fit. They insist on full-time work or nothing.

The tide is turning. A new political climate favours part-time work. Examples of successful conversion of full-time jobs into part-time equivalents are growing. Just because your job has never been done on a part-time basis does not mean that it cannot become part time. My own experience in newspapers is instructive. Newspapers tend to be masculine places and the demands of daily deadlines means that all employees are expected to pull their weight. They are expected to work on any of the seven days of the week and cover almost 24 hours a day. But I have known three different newspaper groups adapting their working practices to allow mothers to cut their working weeks.

Persuading your boss to let you work part time
If you are good at your job most employers would rather keep part of you than have to train someone else. All the effort of interviewing candidates, checking references and instructing a new employee in the way things should be done is off-putting for most bosses.

It is worth doing your homework before putting forward the suggestion that you work part time or share a job. If you want to go part time is there someone else in the office who could fill your role when you are not there? Would the person who stands in for you on maternity leave be willing to keep on doing part of your job? If you provide answers rather than problems, you are likely to be heeded.

How Nicola helped create her own part-time job: *Nicola worked as the export manager for Elida Fabergé in Leeds. It was an exacting job, running an export team which looked after the provision of stock from the* firm's Seacroft factory to the 27 markets supplied by the firm's sister companies.

She had two children aged one and five, but she was seeing less and less of them as her job became more demanding. Her husband also worked long hours as a hospital doctor. The final straw came when her boss asked her to take on more responsibility. She decided to risk her career by asking to go part time.

'It was getting to the point where we couldn't spend any time with the children and I was very unhappy about the whole situation and the children were unhappy and it wasn't right and it wasn't what I wanted. I sat down with my husband and we said: "What are we doing? Where are we going and who are we?"

'We'd given it a four year run in our careers to see who was doing well, who was doing not so well, who was earning the most, who had the best career prospects. We decided that my husband was going to take the lead career and though I'm going to continue with my career I'm also in a supporting role to him. I asked Elida Fabergé if I could go part time.

'I made a case for staying in export logistics which is my function within the company, but working part-time hours by doing a job-share of the export manager role.

'They have accepted me to work part time which is quite a coup because there aren't many part-time workers at Elida Fabergé. I'm not able to stay within my own home function, but I'm prepared for that. I'm going to be assistant category contracts operations manager. It's a role which has not been fully done before. It has been squeezed into the head of production planning's job. It was unthinkable that they could also do that role, as it was a decent size for someone to do part time.'

'This is the Brave New World here, it's a job which has never been done before in a department which has never had a part-time worker before and certainly not a part-time manager. It was brave of Elida Fabergé and I'm very flattered that they want to keep me enough to change my contract. I know not everybody wants or likes part-time workers.

'It means I can work from nine till two and go home and collect my son from school and collect my daughter from the childminder and I will be home to do Oscar's homework and his spellings and get the tea and bath the baby and for everybody to be in a fit state when their father comes home.

'I don't think I could have adapted my old job to part-time working from home because a lot of software I use is network software and is only available in the office. Also, a lot of my job was on the ground talking to *customers, liaising with the factory, going over to the warehouse. It's not the kind of work that can be done from a laptop from home. I don't think doing half a day from home would be acceptable to my employers because the role is very much seen as you are here, you have to take calls from customers.*

'If they need a response you have to be able to work on it now. If you've got a problem with a hairspray and a customer's going out of stock you need to be able to put in place measures to rectify that. You can't really do that from home. You need to be able to see the contracts team, go to the factory, talk to the production managers, talk to the market, get on the phone to Scandinavia. You need to be there with the people and the teams around you to be able to go and chat to them and sort it out. It's quite an operational job.'

Nicola's part-time arrangements still involved her working in the office and factory every day. But there are other variants on part-time working. At Glaxo Wellcome, the pharmaceuticals manufacturer, two senior marketing managers persuaded their bosses to work three days a week instead of five. The firm was open to persuasion because half its UK sales and marketing team are female and it wants to encourage all mothers to return to work.

'In my experience, working mothers are often streets ahead in terms of time management,' said the firm's human resources manager, Ian Brown. 'The two senior marketing managers are working a three-day week yet getting a five-day job done.'

There is, of course, a danger here. If you are getting as much work done part time as you did when you were full time, you should be paid as much as before. Otherwise, it would suit many employers for all their staff to be paid part-time wages if productivity remained the same.

Part-time work from home

Realistically, most of us cannot be as productive working three days as we can working five. However, more and more mothers are reaching arrangements where they work part time in the office and part time at home. There is a strong argument to say that you can get much more done at home because you do not have constant interruptions.

However, do not kid yourself that you will be able to work flat out at home with a baby in the house, unless you have someone else to do the hands-on child care. An au pair, mother's help or grandparent would be fine. You could work when baby is asleep or in the evenings when your partner is there, too, provided you do not have deadlines to meet during the day.

The miracles of e-mail, fax and the Internet are available at low cost and no longer need to dominate a home. A laptop the size of a briefcase can be a home office.

Home programming: *Jill, from Liverpool, works part-time from home as a computer programmer. Her son Nathan is eighteen months old. The company she works for runs a home-shopping catalogue and internet service. The computer systems which control the operation need to be working round the clock and Jill is there to repair the software if things go wrong.*

'I'm part of a standby team,' she said. 'I've got a computer at home and I can work from there remotely.'

To do so, Jill relies on her husband Brian to look after the baby when an emergency happens. She could not concentrate on the computer and Nathan at the same time. 'Most of the time, Jill doesn't get called,' he said, 'but we have to be at home in case. We can't go out and see friends or anything.'

Part-time by supervising a job-sharer

Modern technology makes it easier for many people to job-share. If you are happy to be on the end of a phone on your days off, then the office benefits from having your expertise available. It may be possible for your company to use a junior to do your job when you are not there and for you to be a consultant at the end of the phone. In that way, they get a better deal.

In a large organisation it is likely that there will be two women having babies at similar times who can share a job. But just because other mothers are working full time does not mean that none of them would welcome cutting down their work. It is worth finding out.

It may be possible that your plans will give someone else the opportunity to stretch themselves a couple of days a week by standing in for you – with you at arm's length. Your skills can be extended to others.

One way of selling this to your boss is to remind him or her how difficult it is when you go on holiday. How much has to be put on hold until you return? How much has to be planned in detail before you depart? During your future holidays your deputy will be able to keep things going better than before (when you had no deputy at all).

During non-holiday times you will work three days a week and on your days off you can offer to be 'on call' on a mobile phone in case problems crop up. Under the new system, you will argue, things could run even smoother than before.

Attitudes are changing and many employers are experiencing a skills shortage. With near full employment, many bosses are finding it difficult to recruit. For that reason you hold more aces than you think as you negotiate the way you will work when you get back.

If you make it clear that you will throw yourself in 100 per cent when you are in the office but that you must leave at 5pm without exception, you may be surprised by the response. Your boss and colleagues are more likely to watch the clock than you do. They will want to get you on your way because they will not want to lose you. If you spell out that your childminder or nursery will not look after your child beyond a certain time and that if you lose their services you will be forced to give up work, they will understand. It will help if you always arrive promptly in the morning and are sitting at your desk when your colleagues come in.

Saving work up

In the same way, if you are never there on Mondays or Fridays you will be surprised to find how the working week will be adapted so that the more difficult jobs are done on Tuesday, Wednesday and Thursday. Everyone will get used to planning so that there is work waiting for you on Tuesday mornings that you can get stuck into straight away.

They may even begin to e-mail you at home so you can start thinking of what needs doing the next day before you actually sit down at your desk. This new technology is hugely liberating for working mothers. Unlike a telephone, you do not have to be 'on call'. You can look at your messages when you choose.

It is helpful that the workaholic way of doing business is no longer regarded as the only way. Fathers are just as reluctant to be part of the long hours culture. Older bosses may regret that they did not see more of their children growing up and may quietly admire you for not making the same mistakes.

Part-time work for temps

Even casual or temporary workers can go part time. If you have become a valued worker who knows the routine of the company, your employer is likely to want to retain your skills rather than have to recruit and train someone else.

The temporary worker who went part time: *Lorraine (20) from Hamilton in South Lanarkshire, decided to go part time to have more contact with her three-year-old son Mac and to save money on her nursery costs. She was a full-time 'temporary' clerical worker for the local council, earning £160.50 a week. Her nursery costs were £46.50 a week. They would have been twice that if she had not qualified for a grant from the European Social Fund for young people who have been in care.*

Lorraine's grant was about to end when she applied to work part time. She could not afford the full nursery costs of £93 a week on her income and thought it would be cheaper to look after her son herself for part of the week. She asked the council's one-parent adviser for help. To her delight, her job was converted from temporary to permanent. She was given two increments in pay and told she could work 17½ hours a week and qualify for the new Working Families Tax Credit (you must work more than 16 hours a week to qualify).

'I ended up only about five pounds a week worse off once my benefits were counted in,' she said. 'If I had stayed working full-time in my temporary job, it would have been far worse. I would have had to pay £93 a week in nursery fees. This way, I can look after Mac for two-and-a-half days a week at home, and my nursery costs stay the same. Also I have a permanent job, which is far better than the temporary one I had before.'

Lorraine's employer was generous. Lorraine could have given up work altogether and lived on welfare. Half the working mothers under the age of 25 do so, opting for zero childcare costs and maximum state benefits. Lorraine chose work instead. Now she has the chance of becoming a full-time permanent council worker when her son goes to school.

Discrimination

Many mothers would like to go back to work part time but are refused by employers. Bosses are often worried by what they see as the expense of recruiting a replacement employee to cover the hours when the part-time worker is absent. Some are simply too lazy to re-organise the schedules of existing employees. In one bizarre case, Virgin Atlantic Airways demanded payment from part-time workers for the 'inconvenience' they were causing.

Ordered to pay for going part-time: Linda was working as a part-time steward when Virgin Atlantic altered the terms and conditions of its part-time staff, making them all pay a thousand pounds a year towards the 'administrative costs' of part-time working. The firm continued the policy for two years, then dropped it in the face of continued criticism.

However, when Linda asked for her money back, Virgin Atlantic refused. Linda took the company to an industrial tribunal and Virgin backed down. It paid her about £2,500 in back pay and pensions contributions.

The Equal Opportunities Commission described the case as evidence of how employers 'fail to recognise the valuable contribution part-timers make to the workplace. Part-time working can make it easier for women to return to work after maternity leave and for both men and women to combine work with the care of children or elderly relatives.'

Cases where basic terms and conditions of employment are worse than for full-time workers are relatively easy to take to an industrial tribunal. The facts are usually plain. But some cases of discrimination are more subtle. Part-time workers often complain that they have been passed over for promotion merely because they do not work full time. This is harder to prove, unless a fellow worker with lower qualifications is promoted ahead of you.

There is currently no absolute right to switch from full-time to part-time working after having a baby. But there are voices being raised to change the status quo.

'Employers should be forced to give mothers the legal right to return to decent part-time jobs,' Jane Waldfogel of the London School of Economics told BBC television's *Panorama* programme in January 2000.

'In this country it seems the minute you say you'd like to come to work part time, that sends a signal to the employer that you're not very work-oriented, not very interested in a career. Employers have separate types of jobs that they set aside for those part-time workers, and they're very different from the full-time jobs. They're quite often in different locations, different sectors and they tend to be low-skilled, low-paid and dead-end.

'Women who work part time at a lower grade hardly ever regain their status. In the long run they're going to have lower lifetime earnings, lower pensions and less interesting careers, and in the aggregate the country is wasting all those skills and abilities, they're not making the best use of those women.'

There is a European Directive on part-time work which aims to end discrimination. It does not yet have the force of law. However, mothers may be able to use existing laws on sexual discrimination to bring their employers to heel. There is also an excellent booklet called *Part-time workers, not second class citizens* which is available free from the Equal Opportunities Commission. You can either order it directly from the website (www.eoc.org.uk) or send a letter to:

Customer Contact Point
Equal Opportunities Commission
Overseas House
Quay Street
Manchester M3 3HN.

The booklet is aimed principally at employers. It sets out clearly what their obligations are in terms of:

- access to part-time jobs
- allowing an employee to switch to part-time work
- allowing employees to change their hours
- promoting part-time employees
- ensuring part-time workers get equal pay and conditions
- allowing part-time employees equal access to training
- ensuring part-time employees have equal treatment over maternity leave.

Fathers as part-time workers
The issue of men having access to part-time jobs is assuming great importance, too. One in ten male workers is now doing a part-time job, almost three times more than a decade ago. For many dual-income couples it is the obvious way to share childcare. Even in such male-dominated professions as the police, employers are beginning to back down.

The policeman who won the right to work part time: *Police constable Jeffrey Gilbert was a community beat officer for Thames Valley Police. He asked to go part time for ten months to help look after his three children until his youngest daughter started school. His wife had a demanding job as a hospital operating theatre practitioner.*

He was refused because the force considered childcare was not 'reason enough' to alter his duties. He was warned that his job might be at risk because of his request. But when he took the force to an industrial tribunal

in October 1999, he won. Thames Valley agreed to pay him £2,000 in an
out-of-court settlement a few days before he was due to argue that he had
been the victim of sex discrimination.

There is no reason why fathers in other occupations should not
now request part-time working on similar grounds to those cited by
PC Gilbert. This would take the pressure off mothers enormously,
especially in their second and third pregnancies. Fear of being sued
for sex discrimination may force employers to think of men as potential
joint childcarers instead of cannon fodder who can be bullied into
ignoring their families and working long hours. Good employers are
already encouraging male employees to do this. Littlewoods, for
example, goes so far as to allow fathers to share maternity leave
with their partners. After the birth, the mother may take the first
two months of looking after the baby and the father the second
two months.

2. Flexitime

Flexitime usually involves doing a full-time job but choosing your
hours around a fixed 'core time' which everyone in your department
works. Sometimes, you can choose your own core times but they
must fit the needs of your job. It is very common in local authorities
throughout the UK. For employees, it may involve not just fitting in
childcare on a day-to-day basis, but working longer hours each day and
saving up 'credit hours' which they can take as extra time off at the
end of each month.

Pros and cons
The advantage for employers is that it is much cheaper than part-time
work to adminster because other staff do not need to take over your
job. It also means the employer can cover more hours, an important
consideration for businesses where a longer working day is becoming
standard practice. Some companies have found themselves paying less
overtime as a result of flexitime, because staff don't mind staying late
to finish the job they had started. If they feel in control of their
working day, they will make up the hours they were away with their
children – at standard rates of pay.

All these are powerful arguments, but they may be hard to sell
if you are the only employee in your organisation who wants to

work flexitime. Many bosses find it an effort to have to deal with an exception to their rules. They like the certainty of a standard working day. To adjust to the concept of someone coming and going involves thinking about time in an entirely new way. Often their biggest fear is that the core hours, when the business is at its busiest, will not be covered. Some also worry that it will cost a fortune to sct up an effective method of recording the working hours of flexitime workers.

Again, you must make out a business case, showing how your proposed working pattern would fit in with your colleagues and the needs of your organisation.

The flexible boss: Sharon Field is the customer service manager at the Abbey National's Islington branch in North London. She has dealt with many requests from her staff for flexitime. But the business must come first.

'My key times are all day Friday and all day Monday,' she says. 'I would tell a working mother that she must be available those days. I have one of my staff working nine to five on Mondays and Fridays and then doing 11.30am to 2.30pm on Tuesdays, Wednesdays and Thursdays. It suits both her and the branch.

'Flexitime is great for working mums and for employees who want to take courses. A lot of Abbey National employees choose to work from 9.30am to 2.30pm so they can pick up their children from school. You can work until 8pm at night at this branch. Some staff schedule mortgage interviews between five and eight in the evening and take time off earlier in the day. If the pattern of demand changes, we might have to ask for an employee to work different working hours, but we would still allow flexitime. Often an employee will be contracted to work 1,244 hours a year rather than so many hours a week.'

The very nature of some people's work makes them ideal candidates for flexitime. If you are a social worker, for example, you have to visit clients for part of each day and do the paperwork at other times. It may be possible to do some of the paperwork from home and concentrate your 'core time' on seeing clients, making phone calls on their behalf and attending meetings. The problems arise if too many of your colleagues want the same time off as you do – especially to pick up children from school in the afternoons. Your boss may insist on retaining a percentage of the team to cover emergencies.

It may be that you can ask a childminder to be on 'standby' in case of work emergencies. This means paying her a retainer. If she does have to collect your children, she must be careful not to break the law by having to supervise too many young children.

The mobile telephone has transformed flexitime. Many mothers can now pretend to be working when they are not. Who is to know you are collecting your children when you say you are 'away from your desk'?

3. Job-sharing

A job-share usually means two people sharing one full-time job. You have half the working week free, but you lose half your pay. Job-shares are tricky to arrange if there are no more employees in your line of work. If you are the only brain surgeon in a hospital, it is hard to share that job with another. However, if you are one of five hundred nurses, you stand a very good chance of finding a match. Job-sharing among senior managers is rare, but there is no real reason why even a company director could not job-share, with a little planning and ingenuity.

Pros and cons

The advantage of a job-share to the employer is that your skills and experience are retained. If you choose your partner well, (or your boss finds someone who would make a good match) there can be gains in terms of the range of skills. A job-share also means there is less worry about times of sickness and holidays. When you are absent, at least half a job is being done rather than none. If your job-sharing partner leaves for another job, you are still there to train up the new partner. Continuity is maintained.

The disadvantages include extra work for the employer to find a suitable job-sharing partner, extra training costs, extra administrative costs, and, if the job-share involves working at the same time as your job-sharer, extra space and equipment to accommodate you both. If you have a company car or health insurance or membership of a sports club paid for by your employer, either you have to sacrifice your perks, or your employer has to pay double. This can be a considerable barrier to a job-share.

On a more personal level, there may also be conflicts about measuring your worth and that of your 'twin'. Is one of you doing the less valuable part of the job? Is the other job-sharer getting credit for things you have done?

There are many highly successful job-sharing partnerships, each unique. Some sharers split their responsibilities by taking the parts of the job most suited to them and doing them for two or three days a week. Some mothers share their jobs by doing mornings while their sharer does afternoons. This can be very difficult to co-ordinate especially in jobs where the incoming job-sharer has to be updated on the outgoing sharer's progress.

A more workable arrangement is for job-sharers to take turns doing three days of one week and two days of the next, swapping over every fortnight. However, if you want to work three days permanently, it is often harder to find a partner who only wants two days' work a week. For this reason, many firms insist that each job-sharer works exactly half the week – two-and-a-half days.

If you are in full-time work, finding a job-sharer to take over half your job is easier if you work for a large organisation. The chances of finding someone on your grade or with your skills are so much stronger. It is often a good idea to advertise in your company's house magazine for a job-sharing partner. Use the grapevine to find other mothers who may want to cut back their working hours and who are suitable matches for your kind of job.

Turning a full-time job into a job-share: *Miranda was working full time as a receptionist for a financial services company in Harrow, Middlesex, when she became pregnant. She had been with the firm for three years and asked if she could go part time. Her firm agreed and advertised her job internally as a job-share.*

A temporary worker saw the advertisement and applied for the job, even though she had not been looking for a permanent post. They both agreed to do 17½ hours each week. Miranda worked Mondays, Tuesdays and Wednesday mornings and her job-sharer Anne took the remaining two-and-a-half days.

Her firm, AON Consulting Ltd, brings in a temporary replacement worker if Miranda's baby is ill. Her job-sharer Anne has also covered for her.

Anne said: 'I wasn't thinking of getting a permanent job when I saw the advertisement for a job-share. I was happy temping. But I liked the company and the atmosphere and I decided to go for it – provided I wasn't expected to work outside my 17½ hours.

'There are lots of job-shares around. I had one when I worked in an office as a civil servant and it was very informal, you could swap days off with the other job-sharers. More often than not the more mature people who hadn't got young children were the ones who could help out easiest. I worked in one office where mothers helped each other out a lot. Two of the mothers were friends and they used to look after the other's children when they took their different days off.'

If you have a partner lined up, it saves your employer a great deal of effort and is more likely to enable your job-share to be accepted. But the match must be genuine. You must also be prepared for your job-sharing partner to leave, as the following case demonstrates.

The mothers with parallel careers: *Barbara worked as a supervisor for the Cheshire Health Authority. 'I was in a job share with another girl, for about six years,' she said. 'We were senior supervisors authorising payments and sorting out most of the GP correspondence that comes through. We both got pregnant at the same time and we decided to come back part time. We were on the same level at the time. We got promoted together too. We'd worked together for quite a long time and we knew each other's way of working, we complemented each other.*

'We worked 18½ hours a week, but shared it between us so we did three days/two days alternately. We did it to save money on childcare. We never had any problems.'

The arrangement worked well until her partner, Liz, decided to go on secondment to another department. Barbara went back to full-time working even though her son Martin was only nine months old. It also coincided with the breakdown of her marriage.

'I'm a single parent now. My daughter Lucy had just started school when I went full time, so I needed a childminder to look after Martin. The childminder does three days a week, then my mum and dad do two days a week. I work Monday to Friday full time. It's what the job involves. I've got two teams under me and I've got to be here between the core times five days a week. Our organisation is very compassionate. If you've got a flexible employer you're half way there.'

In theory, there are very few jobs unsuitable for job-sharing. The former Social Security Secretary Harriet Harman has even suggested that government ministers could job-share. She had school-age children herself while she was a cabinet minister and with nearly 40 female ministers in the British government, she wants more flexibility.

In 1999, she suggested that Yvette Cooper, the Minister for Public Health and Jacqui Smith, the Schools' Minister, who both had young children, could job-share. They could, she said, spend half their time in their departmental posts and half on the back benches of the House of Commons. Ms Harman claimed it would be no more expensive because they could share an office and a car, even though they worked for different ministries.

She said: 'In the world outside, women work part time, they work flexitime and some do job-shares. But in the Government, nothing has changed and women are still expected to work like men whose family responsibilities remain with their wives. As part of the modernisation process, there should be more flexibility about how people can be ministers.'

4. Twilight working

A 'twilight' working shift between 4pm and 9pm has been introduced by the National Insurance Contributions Office (NICO) in Newcastle to allow working mothers to co-ordinate childcare with their male partners.

It is common in call centres because an increasing number of customers prefer to telephone banks, travel agencies or similar services once they have finished their nine-to-five jobs. A twilight shift is only feasible, however, if you have someone else to look after your children in the early evening.

'A lot of men work shifts in Newcastle,' says Dawn Jarvis, the equal opportunities manager for NICO. 'The idea is for their wives to work the opposite shift but still manage to pick the children up from school. If their husbands are on nights, they finish their shift at six in the morning and go home to sleep. A lot of them pick the kids up from school in the afternoon while their wives start work on the twilight shift. It means the wives are back home in time to take over the childcare.'

Many mothers in other parts of the country are also taking advantage of evening shifts.

Dad takes over: Jackie has two children, Oliver, aged four and a baby daughter, Jemima. She lives in a small town in Essex and gave up her old job when she realised her salary as the PA to the managing director of a fashion company would not cover childcare and her commuting costs.

She found a job in a call centre for the local electricity company. She applied, took an English and maths test and got the job.

'My daughter was only six weeks old when I started. I had to do five nights a week from 6pm to 11pm. It was too much. But I have been there two years now and I have reduced it to four nights a week – Sunday, Monday, Wednesday and Thursday all year round.'

'My husband is a builder and he leaves work at five in the morning and is always back by five in the evening. In two years he's only been late once. It is lovely for the children that he can do everything for them that I can do. He is much more involved than most fathers.'

5. Weekend working

An increasing number of businesses are now open at weekends to improve their service to customers. It also allows parents to work while their partners care for the children.

Lloyds TSB, like many banks, now offers telephone banking seven days a week, round the clock. It sees flexibility of working patterns as critical to retaining a competitive edge.

Some employees who have childcare duties throughout the week have the opportunity at weekends to hand over to their partners. They can work over the weekend instead.

The couple who take turns in childcare: *Jill has two pre-school children aged six months and two years. She could not afford to work and pay for a childminder. Her husband Ian is a full-time accountancy student. He earns money by working in the student bar three evenings a week, but his income is not enough to cover their weekly spending.*

Jill saw an advertisement for work at the Lloyds TSB telephone banking callcentre. She applied and got a job working two twelve-hour shifts on Saturday and Sunday.

'It's perfect for us,' said Jill. 'Ian looks after our son and daughter while I go off to work on Saturday morning. It's only for a couple of years until Ian qualifies.'

6. Term-time working

A vast range of businesses in Britain now allow some of their employees to fit in with the school holidays. They include banks such as Barclays and Abbey National, retailers such as W H Smith, Littlewoods and Boots, health authorities such as the Greenwich Healthcare Trust and the Bethlem and Maudsley NHS Trust and manufacturing companies such as Zeneca Pharma.

School holidays vary from one part of the country to the next, so contracts have to be adjusted every year to fit. The idea is to take unpaid leave during school holiday times. Paid annual leave is also taken during school holiday periods. For most employees, this means that around nine weeks of the year are unpaid.

Pros and cons

The main advantage to the employer is that it attracts able women with school-age children who would normally be lost to the employment market. The disadvantages are a small increase in administrative costs to deal with varying school holidays, the need to recruit replacement workers for holiday periods and the resentment of permanent staff at having to cover for their colleagues' absence.

If your job cannot easily be done by a temporary replacement or your deputy, term-time working may be ruled out if the business cannot run properly during the six to nine weeks of the year when you would be unavailable for work. A way round this might be to offer your 'consultancy services' from home. You may, for example, be able to do part of your job from your spare bedroom with a computer and a telephone.

Some firms have planned their working year around school terms so that they can attract able working mothers. It works best for businesses where work is fairly predictable.

The company that built itself around school holidays: *Market Monitor, based in the small Buckinghamshire town of Princes Risborough, owns and maintains a UK business database for use by other businesses' marketing departments. It employs 26 people, 18 of whom work only during school term times.*

'All the mothers we employ have children of school age,' says Mary Clements, the database manager of Market Monitor. 'They often start when their children go to school. They all come into our offices rather than working from home, partly because they work better that way and also because mothers want to get out of the house when their children are at school. There's a social aspect to it.

'We do very high quality work. We have researchers who telephone businesses and ask them for information and we have inputters who

convert the information so that it fits the database. The two teams of people need to interact, so it makes sense for them to be together. We also get greater consistency of work.

'Most start off on reduced hours. They will work 9am–1pm or 1pm–3pm for 39 weeks a year. They get pro-rata benefits.'

The company covers school holidays by employing students to stand in for the term-time staff. It says this approach is economical because recruitment costs are kept to a minimum. Most students ask for work after hearing about the company from friends. They join for two to three years' worth of holiday working, so that training costs are also kept to a minimum.

'Some of our term-time workers come back for two weeks during the school holidays,' says Mary Clements. 'It is up to them. It works very well in Princes Risborough because travelling distances are very short, so that coming in to work for three or four hours is no big problem.'

7. School-hours working

This often goes hand-in-hand with term-time working. Many employers allow parents to work hours which fit in with collecting children from school. For example, a shift may start at 9.30am and end at 2.30 pm, to allow an employee to take the children to school and travel to work.

Teleworking is particularly suited to school hours. For example, some mothers work at their employer's premises in the morning and from home in the evening, leaving afternoons free for childcare. If you work entirely from home (see 9. Working from home, page 89) it is even easier to split your working day.

Unpredictable jobs are not usually suited to school-hours working. Your absence can place a big burden on your colleagues, as the case of this Birmingham social worker makes plain.

The social worker who put her own child first: *Jane had a tough job as a social worker in a fostering unit. She often had work crises to deal with that conflicted with her role as the adoptive parent of three school-age children. The Adoption Panel had made it a condition that she should only work a two-and-a-half day week.*

She said: 'If I was in the office at two in the afternoon and the child I was supervising as a social worker had a crisis, I either had to look at my watch and think 'Am I going to get this finished by three o'clock? If I am I'll do it.' If not, I'd have to go to a colleague and say "Can you do this for me because there's no way I'm going to be finished by three o'clock, I've got the kids to pick up from school."

Jane solved her problem by being open. She would telephone the school and bargain with the headmistress to look after her children while she dealt with a crisis. She would also bargain with her clients.

'Foster carers would phone me up and say "You've got to come out, he's driving me mad. He's run away" and it would be five to three. I would say, look I've got to pick up my kids from school, can I get them home, wait for my husband and I'll come over later this evening and they would say "Yes that's fine, as long as you're going to come at some point today." It's the nature of being a social worker.

'Had I worked as a receptionist for BT and I was told your hours are going to be from nine till three, it would have been easy. I had my own case-load so it was always asking somebody to do my work. It's a bit like being a GP who has her own patients and is getting her colleagues to cover for her.'

Jane found her unmarried colleagues the least sympathetic to her problems. 'It wasn't that they were being unfair or unsupportive, they just really didn't understand. One of those colleagues has subsequently had two children and she says: "How many more times do you want me to say sorry for the hard times I used to give you?" Those without children really don't understand that you need to go into school because your kid's in trouble or ill. They used to be thinking to themselves: "Why can't you just leave?" You could almost see it on their faces.

'My husband was a great help. He's an engineer and he's managed to get his firm to support him when he needs to take over from me. We sort out holidays and half terms between us. When I work late he comes home early to look after my youngest who is thirteen, makes her tea and takes her to Guides. It's very much done between us. Sometimes I can't go to school for the children and he says: "That's all right, I'll go".'

8. Compressed hours working

Squashing a working week into four or four-and-a-half days means you can spend more time with your children – or share childcare with your partner.

There are other variations of compressed hours such as the nine-day fortnight or even the three- or three-and-a-half-day week. It depends very much on the nature of your job. A twelve-hour shift is simply not relevant to many kinds of work; an employer would therefore be unlikely to let you do it.

The advantages of compressed hours working to your employer are that there is little or no extra administration involved and productivity is unlikely to be affected. If everyone is expected to work a four-and-a-half-day week, your employer might even make a saving in terms of the cost of heating, lighting and other overheads.

The disadvantage of compressed hours working is that you have to find someone who can cover the extra hours you work on your main days. Finishing work at six in the evening is often too late for many nurseries. You must weigh up the cost of having someone collect your child on your behalf against the gain of having time off at the end of the week.

Three-day weekends: *Julie works for a family doctor on the outskirts of Glasgow. She has compressed her 38-hour working week into four days to give her more time with her daughter. She starts work at 7.45am and finishes at 5.15pm every Monday, Tuesday, Wednesday and Thursday. She then has three days off with her husband John, who works a 28-hour week.*

'It means we can have time with our daughter,' says John. 'I don't see the point of having kids unless you're going to have some input into their lives. The only bad part is having to leave her on Mondays with someone else.'

The nine-day fortnight: *Catherine was working full-time as a microbiologist in Leeds when her daughter was born. She continued full-time working when she returned, 29 weeks after Bethany was born. Both sets of grandparents took turns to look after Bethany. Catherine could not afford to lose income. She was also afraid that she might not be considered for promotion if she went part time, but she did want to see more of her daughter.*

She switched to a four-day, 40-hour week with every Friday off. Another mother in the same department also switched to four-day working but took Mondays off each week instead. The two working patterns dovetailed.

'It was great going out with Bethany on Fridays,' said Catherine. 'I'd take her to playgroups, visit friends with other young children. It was a fun day out for both of us. The problem was that it was getting late by the time I got home on the other days. I'd miss tea and bedtime by the time I got home. Also I found it a bit restrictive always having the same day off each week.'

Finally, when Bethany was two, Catherine hit on another solution – a nine-day fortnight. She worked from eight till five every day, working alternately a full week and a four-day week.

'I could take my day off on any day within the fortnight. It gave me much more flexibility. If I've got a medical appointment for Bethany I can take the day off, or a Christmas party or my friends coming over. I get home at a very reasonable hour, the same as everyone else, about half past five. It's up to me to pick my day off. If I plan it and tell my boss a couple of days before and mark it on the office calendar, everyone's happy.'

The four-and-a-half-day week: *Dawn persuaded her boss to let her work four days instead of five in the office and work for three hours from home every Friday so that she could be with her baby daughter, Jessie.*

'The deal was that I had to work longer hours during my four days in the office,' she said. 'I'd still put Jessie in the nursery as if I was working in the office, but in the afternoon, I'd go and pick her up and spend the afternoon with her. As long as I put the hours in, it was fine by my boss.'

Dawn works as the Equal Opportunities Manager at the National Insurance Contributions Office in Newcastle where many of the staff work flexitime.

'You can do five days' work over four days if you want to. You work longer each day. But the business must come first. If you can produce for your manager a working pattern that works for you and the business feels it can support that, then anything will be considered. If your work starts to suffer, for example if you're coming off maternity leave and you want to do three part-time days, if the whole workforce works those days and we need people in on a Thursday and Friday we'd say no. We wouldn't let you take those days because we would still need to support our customers. But we will support where we can, so long as it's feasible.'

9. Working from home

The computer revolution has transformed home working, especially in the past ten years with the rise of the internet. Many mothers can now take work home and be with their children instead of staying late in the office. One firm, Rank Xerox, went so far as to ask twenty senior managers to work from home in the early 1980s so that it could sell an expensive office block in the centre of London.

In my own field, journalism, there are thousands of mothers working from home, fitting in childcare while researching and writing articles. Some structure their work patterns around school hours, writing when the children have gone to bed. Most use some kind of childcare too, especially childminders, nurseries and grandparents.

The computer has made this pattern of working possible because articles can now be sent by e-mail. In the past, their work would have been sent by post or laboriously dictated over the telephone.

Mother and full-time journalist: *Annie was a freelance showbusiness and financial reporter working from home in Brighton before she had her daughter, Emma. At first, she needed to keep earning as much as she could to establish her career, so she employed a live-out nanny. It meant that Emma could be cared for when she went out on assignments or for meetings in London.*

When Emma started school, however, Annie decided she could manage the childcare herself. She switched fields, doing more magazine and internet work which involved less travel. Her husband, Derek, often works nights. If she has to go away, either he, a childminder or a friend will collect Emma from school.

'I am there most days,' says Annie. 'A lot more work can be done on the computer now than when I first became a freelance. I just have to organise my day so that I am free at three o'clock every afternoon. Emma is ten now, so it is easier to leave her with friends.'

Many other information-based jobs can now be done by computers. If you have basic secretarial skills you have the opportunity to become a full-time mother and earn a living at the same time.

Three children and a new career: *Jill worked as a secretary for a London firm of chartered surveyors until she had her first child eleven years ago. She did not want to attempt commuting while looking after a small baby, so she investigated an entirely new field – publishing.*

Through networking and word-of-mouth, she found work preparing manuscripts for authors and corporate publishing – including her old firm. She had to buy her own computer when her son was four months old. Within three months it had paid for itself. She would type while he slept. Over the next year she was given steady work. She took on a couple of large projects for healthcare companies which required her to organise linguists and data-inputters. All of it could be done on the telephone from home.

She charges from £9 to £12 an hour and works from 8.30am to 3.30pm. Sometimes she starts again when the children, now aged eleven, nine and seven, are in bed. She has been able to take all three to school every day. She is a school governor.

'I love it,' she said. 'I am very organised. I get a great sense of satisfaction in knowing that I can get things done when I want to. I have 15 clients, 10 of whom are very regular. Since Christmas I have been offered work by three new firms but I had to turn them down as I do not have the time to take their work on.'

During holidays, Jill often has local teenagers to help out with her children, but she is always there to supervise. She tries to schedule work around holidays but finds that Christmas is a difficulty as the firms she works for do not slow down and do not close down for three weeks like schools.

'One of the problems is educating friends that I am working. They sometimes call round and do not perceive what I do as real work. They think I have all day to drink coffee and chat. I have to say I am actually working.'

Some businesses are building entire teams around 'teleworking' from home. The Automobile Association, for example, has gradually transferred more and more call-centre staff to teleworking. From a pilot scheme involving 10 staff in 1997, the initiative now involves 60 employees and there are plans to expand it to 150. Teleworkers are about 30% more productive than their call-centre counterparts.

'This is not a replacement for childcare,' said Denise Raven of the AA in Leeds. 'Our teleworkers still work a structured shift. We make sure their homes have a private place where they can be separate from the family as much for health and safety reasons as anything else. They still need childcare, but wherever possible we let them structure their shifts so that they can look after their children for part of the day themselves.'

The teleworker who splits her day: *Paula works six hours a day as an AA teleworker from the spare bedroom of her house in Leeds. It means she can take her two children Abbey, aged eleven and Joel, aged four, to and from school every day.*

Previously, when Abbey was a toddler, she had worked on the morning shift at the AA's local call-centre and had to ferry her husband and child around in the car.

'I had to get Abbey up at the crack of day,' she said. 'I would take my husband to work so that I could have the car. Then I would take Abbey to the nursery for 8am. In the afternoons I would pick her up from the nursery at 1.45pm, take her home and then pick my husband up when he finished work. I was travelling six miles in the morning and six miles at night. Abbey used to sleep in the car a lot.'

Now Paula works from home. She does a split shift, three hours in the morning from 8am to 11am and three hours in the evening from 4pm to 7pm.

'I take them to school in my morning break at 8.45. I'm meant to have ten minutes but my supervisor says if I take longer there's no problem, I can make up the lost time at the end of the shift. So long as I do six hours, no-one is worried.'

For teleworkers with older children, there is not the need to split shifts because the children can bring themselves home. There can be big financial gains.

The teleworker who doubled her pay: *Annette worked full time at a call centre. But her shift pattern made childcare difficult. Every six weeks she worked nights. She would take her two children Victoria and Christopher to nursery and to school the morning after her night shift and snatch a few hours of sleep in between bringing them home or taking them to their grandmother's house.*

She found the strain too much and went part time so that she could have every afternoon and evening off to look after them. But her pay went down.

'I was doing 20 hours a week. When the chance of teleworking came up, I realised that I could look after my children and work full time again.'

Annette now works from 11.30 in the morning until 5.30 in the evening from the dining room of her home. Her children can come straight home from school, where tea is waiting. If there is an emergency, her mother can break off work and deal with it. With overtime, she is earning almost double her part-time salary.

'The kids think it's wonderful that mum's at home because they can come here straight from school instead of having to be collected by someone else and stay with them until my husband finishes at six in the evening,' she said.

'The only downside is loneliness. I miss the banter and the gossip of being in a call centre. I've been doing the job for nine months and it's getting easier. At first I didn't like it because I'm quite chatty, but now I'm more motivated. If I'm finding things a problem I can always change my hours.'

10. A career break
A career break is costly, unless you have a very generous employer. Not only do you lose your income, but, with a baby to look after, you spend

more, too. Children do not come cheap. They eat, they drink, they wear clothes, they use nappies. They need gadgets for travelling, gadgets for staying still – cots, buggies, high chairs, low chairs, car seats, harnesses, baby alarms – which all cost money.

What is more, children grow. No sooner have you bought one set of kit and clothing than you need a new, larger, more expensive version to keep pace with their development. If you do not have a partner to pay the bills, you can be in big financial trouble very quickly.

Most working mothers are afraid of taking a career break for financial reasons. The 1999 Johnson and Johnson survey of first-time mothers showed that most mothers returned to work because they said they could not afford the 'luxury' of staying at home. They also thought it was socially 'frowned upon' to choose to be a full-time mother and many believed working mothers were now too embarrassed to give up their careers to stay at home.

This assumes, of course, that a career break means giving up work altogether. But it does not have to be all or nothing. A few mothers are staying at home and paying their own way by taking part-time work which better fits the demands of childcare.

A career break is not easy. You must have an enlightened employer who will promise to keep your job open and keep that promise when you return. Most British employers do not do so, despite the growing evidence that they would save money in the long term by reducing their organisations' retraining and recruitment costs.

Without written guarantees that you can resume work at the same level as when you left, it is too risky to take a career break and expect to take up where you left off. Even those with specialist skills, such as nurses or accountants, cannot merely assume that they will be welcomed back into their old jobs – unless they have it in writing. Even two years is a long time to be away from work. Your old employer will almost certainly want you to go through some retraining to get you back up to scratch. The National Audit Office holds annual refresher courses for employees on career breaks. It may be some time before your earning levels reach the equivalent of your old job.

A career break is sensible, however, if you either have a working partner who can pay the bills until you go back to work, or if you can find part-time work which you can do from home and look after your children at the same time.

The number of homeworking jobs career-breakers can take is increasing every year. Teleworking, in particular, has made this more and more commonplace. The danger is that you will be sidetracked and that your part-time job will become full time.

The aim of a career break is not to start another career. Some employers forbid their employees to take other paid work while on a career break. A few have lost good staff who used the break to test the market. That is not the point. Any job you do is to supplement your income while you raise the children. It is to tide you over until you go back to your main employment. If your part-time job begins to become something more time-consuming, however, you must sit back and take stock. Is your new line of work better than the one you had? Are you spending more time doing your part-time job than bringing up your children? If so, what have you gained by your career break? Would you not be better off returning to your previous job and paying a childminder or a nanny to look after your children instead of pretending that your new life is genuinely putting the children first?

Back to work by staying at home: *Di was working as a human resources manager for Lloyds TSB when she gave birth to her daughter, Laura, in 1996. She could have taken a career break of five years if she had wanted, and still returned to the same grade. She chose to take a three-year break instead, returning when Laura started at a pre-school nursery.*

During her break she was a full-time mother. She had help from Laura's grandmother who travelled by train to help for days at a time. When Di moved house, grandma came too, selling her house and moving into a flat in Di's home. But by the time Di decided to return to work, she felt it would be too much of a burden for her mother to look after Laura full time.

She asked Lloyds TSB if she could split her old job between home and office as a way of easing her way back into full-time work and spending time with her daughter. The company agreed because her job involved projects and policy matters rather than leading a team. One of her projects was to look after graduate entrants to the bank.

'I was lucky I had a supportive boss,' she said. 'It was the same boss as when I left so there were no problems about not being known. About three months before I wanted to go back I contacted him and we discussed how it could work out. At first I worked two days from home and now I work three days from home. He doesn't mind when I work, so long as I make up the hours. It can be eight in the morning or ten at night.'

Work options – at a glance

1. Part-time working

Keeping your job but working far fewer hours, or switching jobs to
one which needs only a few hours' work each day. There is no right
to convert a full-time job into a part-time one. The advantage to your
employer is that it retains your expertise and cuts down on the cost of
recruiting, training and supervising a replacement. The disadvantage
is it costs more in administration and time management. You lose
pay. Variations include supervising a junior job-sharer from home
on days off.

2. Flexitime

Full-time working but choosing your hours around a fixed 'core time'
which everyone in your department works. The advantage to your
employer is that your skills are retained full time. The business can
cover more hours and pay less overtime. The advantage to you is that
you can take time off outside the core hours and make up the difference
later. You do not lose pay. The disadvantage is that it costs your
employer more in time management systems.

3. Job-sharing

Two people sharing one full-time job. Your employer retains your
skills and can cover your holidays and days off through illness easier.
You gain by having more free time. You lose pay. Your employer may have
to recruit and train your job-sharer, pay for extra space and equipment
if you work simultaneously, pay out extra for health insurance and
other perks.

4. Twilight working

Part-time work in the evening, usually 4–9pm or 5–10pm. It suits
working mothers who can co-ordinate a handover with their partners.
Not available in many industries. Not suitable for many jobs.

5. Weekend working

Part-time work from Friday evenings to Sunday evenings. Allows
working mothers whose partners work conventional five-day weeks
to share childcare and earn an income. Ideal for mothers on career
breaks with limited budgets.

6. Term-time working

Work which fits the school terms and allows every school holiday as unpaid leave. Allows working mothers to avoid heavy childcare costs during holiday periods. Approximately 40 weeks' paid work per year. Advantage to employers is that it attracts able women with school-age children. Some businesses may have to recruit temporary workers to cover for school holidays.

7. School hours working

Work which fits around the school day. Often goes hand-in-hand with term-time working. Advantage to employer is its attraction to able women with school-age children. Disadvantage is that many jobs are unsuited because of their unpredictability.

8. Compressed hours working

Squashing a working week into four or four-and-a-half days. Means working longer hours on main days. Advantage to employer of reducing overheads if everyone takes Friday afternoons off. Disadvantage to you if your childcarer cannot cope with such long hours.

9. Working from home

May be combined with some time at employer's premises. Childcare still needed for most working mothers but less need for trained help. Mother's helps may be able to cope under supervision. Especially suited to information-based jobs. Some call centres now offer home-working.

10. Career break

Absence from full-time work for several years to look after young children. Some employers offer up to five years' career breaks. You must obtain written guarantee of your old job back or equivalent. Unpaid, therefore you need another source of income. Available only for specific jobs and specific grades of worker. Some retraining may be needed. Problems of loss of status and seniority.

5: KNOW YOUR RIGHTS

British people do not have 'constitutional rights' like the citizens of the USA. We have no written constitution which spells out what we can or cannot expect as citizens. Instead we have laws drafted by various parliaments, both national and European, which may change with each government and which are subject to interpretation and definition by the courts.

A typical case in point is the new European Part-Time Work Directive which gives all EC citizens the 'right' to part-time work on equivalent terms and conditions compared with full-time workers. However, it leaves it up to each government to draft national laws to bring justice for part-time workers. The British Government attempted to do so, and was immediately accused of watering down the directive's intent.

As a working mother, you must be alert to what such changes in the law mean to your basic entitlements. You must also find out what extras your employer may be offering above and beyond the legal requirements.

Your duty is to find out what is included in your own contract of employment. If you belong to a trade union, you may be able to get help in interpreting the information. You should do this homework preferably before you get pregnant. That way you can maximise both your maternity leave and your maternity pay.

In Chapter 18, you will see what 'family-friendly' employers offer both mothers and fathers who work for them. These, however, are long-term goals. They are what you and your colleagues can aspire to, not necessarily what you may persuade your boss to do for you before you give birth.

In the meantime, you should know your basic rights, the minimum standards which your employer must follow.

Maternity: your right to time off

Antenatal Care

All pregnant employees are entitled to time off to keep antenatal appointments made on the advice of a doctor, a midwife or a health visitor. Antenatal care can include not only medical examinations but also relaxation classes and parentcraft classes.

Except in the case of your first appointment, you must be prepared to show your employer:

- a certificate from a doctor, midwife or health visitor confirming that you are pregnant
- an appointment card or another document showing that an appointment has been made.

You should be paid your normal hourly rate of pay by your employer when you go to antenatal appointments and you cannot be unreasonably refused permission to go.

If you are in the police or your contract of employment states that you should normally work abroad, you do not have a right to take time off for antenatal care. Your employer can grant you such privileges, however. An industrial tribunal can order your employer to pay compensation if you are refused time off for antenatal appointments or your pay is suspended for attending such classes, provided you complain within three months.

18 Weeks' ordinary maternity leave

You must take at least two weeks' maternity leave after the birth of your child. You have a right to 18 weeks' ordinary maternity leave, which can start eleven weeks before your baby is due. This applies whether you are working full time or part time as a recent case in Northumberland showed.

Wrongly denied maternity leave: *Heather Carmichael and Janet Leese worked for up to 25 hours as part-time guides at Blyth power stations in Northumberland. Their employer, National Power, tried to claim they were not entitled to maternity leave or holiday pay because they worked 'on a casual basis'. But the Court of Appeal ruled in March 1998 that they had entered into contracts by signing and returning letters accepting their jobs.*

The words 'on a casual basis' in the letters did not negate the women's rights, said the judge, who added that it would be 'wholly artificial to treat the applicants as independent contractors'. National Power was ordered to pay costs and leave for an appeal to the House of Lords was refused.

It does not matter how long you have worked for your current boss or whether you were pregnant when you started work – you are still entitled to ordinary maternity leave. But you must tell your employer (preferably in writing) that you are pregnant, 21 days before you want your maternity leave to start. If you want additional maternity leave (see below), you must mention it in the same letter. You must also tell your boss in writing when your baby is due. You must include in the letter a statement that you expect to return to work. You can start your maternity leave at any time from the eleventh week before your baby is due.

You can start your maternity leave six weeks before the birth without telling your employer you are pregnant, if you choose. However, you must tell your boss that you are absent from work wholly or partly because of pregnancy as soon as is 'reasonably practicable'. The same principle applies if you give birth prematurely before you have told your employer that you are pregnant. You must tell your boss what has happened.

Additional maternity leave

If you choose, you can have an extra period of maternity leave lasting 29 weeks from the birth of your child. You qualify only if you have worked for the same employer for a year and you did not conceive your baby earlier than six months into your new job (at the eleventh week before your expected week of childbirth).

You must claim it at the beginning of your ordinary leave by saying in your letter that you are pregnant. In theory, therefore, you can take a maximum of 40 weeks off work if you begin your ordinary maternity leave eleven weeks before your baby is due. To qualify for additional maternity leave, you must also give 21 days' notice of when you want to return. Your employer may find the date you have chosen inconvenient and can delay it by up to four weeks, provided it falls within the maternity leave period.

You are entitled to alternative work or time off on full pay if your job is hazardous and you are currently pregnant, gave birth within the last six months or are still breastfeeding. Under pre-1994 law it was

not unfair dismissal for an employer to fire a pregnant woman who
was not able to do her work because of Health and Safety regulations.
Such a dismissal would now be automatically unfair. It is also unfair to
make a mother-to-be switch jobs because of health and safety fears,
unless a proper risk assessment is carried out as a recent case against
Suffolk Police showed.

*Sidelined because her fitness to work was not assessed: In 1988
Caroline Tapp, a 26-year old police recruit, won her sex discrimination
case against her employers after she was forced to leave a physically
rigorous training scheme which would have won her better pay. Senior
officers learned that she was pregnant and sidelined her to a clerical job.
She was made to restart her training course after the birth of her child,
a decision which lost her £1,000 in annual pay.*

*Caroline argued that she was extremely fit. She trained at the gym
three times a week. But her superiors were worried that the course might
harm her baby. It included riot training and she would have been seven
months pregnant by the end of the course.*

*The tribunal panel ruled that Caroline had suffered sex discrimination.
They said a risk assessment should have been carried out to see what a
pregnant woman was capable of doing so that she could have continued
if she had wished.*

Parental Leave

This is a new right to take 13 weeks off work to look after a child or
make arrangements for your child to be cared for until he or she is
five years old. It applies to any parent, male or female, provided the
child was born or adopted on or after 15 December 1999, the day when
the regulations started. The cut-off date was challenged in the High
Court by the Trades Union Congress, represented by Cherie Booth QC,
the wife of the British Prime Minister, only three days before she
gave birth to her fourth child, Leo. She argued that 2.7 million British
parents had been unfairly deprived of parental leave. The case was
referred to the European Court of Justice and a final verdict is expected
in 2002.

You have a right to 13 weeks' unpaid leave for each of your
children if you have been in your present job for at least a year. It
applies to part-time as well as full-time employees. If you have twins,

you are entitled to 26 weeks' unpaid leave. A child's father who is named on the birth certificate is automatically regarded as having 'parental responsibility'. Other partners may have to show proof that they are a child's legal guardian. Adopters automatically come into this category.

You can take parental leave in chunks of between one and four weeks a year until each child is five. You must give your employer 21 days' notice before each leave, but your boss can postpone it for up to six months if he or she can demonstrate that it will disrupt the running of the business. Unless your company offers a paid parental leave scheme, you will have to save up to cover the cost of your absence. In other countries such as Germany and Sweden where parental leave is unpaid, very few employees take it up.

You could, theoretically, add four weeks of it onto your maternity leave if you chose, giving you a legal entitlement to a maximim of 44 weeks, once additional maternity leave is taken into account. However, this is risky. You lose some privileges if you do so. You are not entitled to your old job back if it is 'not reasonably practicable' for your employer to permit you to do so. You may have to settle for another job which is 'suitable' and 'appropriate' for you to do. Your employer must not, however, give you a pay cut or offer worse conditions of service, or lesser seniority or pension rights.

If your child is entitled to disability living allowance, you can take parental leave until his or her eighteenth birthday. If you adopt children, you can take parental leave up to five years after the placement begins or, if the child is disabled, up to its eighteenth birthday.

Parental leave is a right whether or not it is in your work contract or has been negotiated by a trade union. If you or your partner take less than four weeks' parental leave, you are entitled to return to the job you had before. However, if you take more than four weeks' parental leave, an employer can insist that you change jobs, providing the new job suits your abilities and circumstances.

There is no separate right to paternity leave but employers who offer it usually pay their employees to take it. It comes under the terms of parental leave. Before the new parental leave rules were introduced, about a third of all British employers who had men on their payroll offered paternity leave, usually paid and lasting up to four days. Some employers such as Littlewoods offered ten days' paid paternity leave.

Employment rights

The right not to be unfairly dismissed

You cannot be fired or made redundant solely or mainly because you are pregnant or you have given birth, or for any other reason connected with your pregnancy or childbirth. This applies up to the end of your statutory maternity leave period of 18 weeks, or up to a maximum of four weeks after the end of that period if you have not been able to work because you have a medically-certified illness. It also applies regardless of your length of service.

You are protected against dismissal for taking additional maternity leave without your employer's permission, for refusal to sign a workforce agreement about parental leave or for reasons of health and safety.

The right to have your job back

When you go back to work after statutory maternity leave (18 weeks) you are entitled to have the same or a similar job and the same terms and conditions as if you had not been absent. This does not apply if you are made redundant during your absence.

If you are made redundant during your maternity leave, you are entitled to be offered alternative employment with a new contract – if there is a 'suitable available vacancy'. This applies even if your old company has been taken over by a rival, or your part of the company has been closed down. The new job must be appropriate to your skills and the terms and conditions should not be substantially worse than those of your old job. If you are made redundant, it may be worth taking advice from a lawyer, the Citizens' Advice Bureau or the Equal Opportunities Commission.

If you return after additional maternity leave (up to 40 weeks), you are also entitled to have the same job and the same terms and conditions as if you had not been absent, unless a 'redundancy situation' has arisen during your absence or your employer has a reason why it is not 'reasonably practicable' for you to have your original job back. In such circumstances, you are entitled to be offered suitable alternative work which must be offered before your existing contract runs out. This includes a vacancy with an 'associated employer' or a 'successor to the original employer.'

The alternative work must be both 'suitable and appropriate' for you. It should be no less favourable to you than if you had continued to be employed under your original contract. You are entitled to compensation if you are downgraded. The manager of a luxury shoe department in a large store was awarded almost £4,000 compensation when she was offered a job as an ordinary sales assistant in the sports shoe section.

Part-time work

There is no right to return to work part time if you were employed full time before your maternity leave.

However, in 1999 a parliamentary select committee recommended that women should be guaranteed this right. They said women should receive the same pay and benefits as they did before they went on maternity leave and retain the right to transfer to part-time work. It recommended that employers should be exempted if they could prove that these requirements would harm their business. These recommendations are not yet law but if you make a request to go part time, your employers risk a sex discrimination case if they refuse your request unreasonably.

The Government has devised a code of practice for employers which spells out what a reasonable request includes. You can see it on the Department for Education and Employment's website (www.dfee.gov.uk). Small employers are less likely to be considered unreasonable if they refuse a request for part-time employment than large employers.

Part-time workers are entitled to be treated no less favourably in their terms and conditions of employment than their full-time colleagues.

Dismissals on grounds unrelated to an employee's pregnancy or childbirth

It is not unlawful for an employer to dismiss you on grounds largely or wholly unrelated to your pregnancy or childbirth, unless the dismissal is unfair for some other reason or amounts to discrimination on grounds of sex or marriage.

If you are sacked while you are pregnant or on statutory maternity leave your employer must give you an accurate written statement of the reasons. You do not have to request the statement and the right applies regardless of your length of service. However, if you do request the statement and your employer fails to comply, you could claim compensation from an Industrial Tribunal.

Money – your entitlements

Maternity pay and maternity allowance

You can get 'statutory maternity pay' if you earn more than £67 a week and have worked for your current employer for 26 weeks by the 15th week before the baby is due. In other words, you are entitled if you do not conceive until the second week after starting a new job.

For six weeks your maternity pay will be at 90 per cent of your average earnings and then at a flat rate for twelve weeks (£60.20 a week in 2000). It is taxable. The amount changes annually, so check with your local benefit office. If you do not qualify for statutory maternity pay, you can claim maternity allowance from the DSS if you have paid 26 weeks' National Insurance contributions during the 66 weeks before the expected week of birth. It is not taxable. If you cannot get either, then you may be able to claim other benefits from the DSS.

You are not paid your normal wages during ordinary maternity leave, unless your employer chooses to do so. Your contractual rights such as pensions and holidays continue as if you were still working.

Child Benefit

Child Benefit is payable to anyone bringing up a child under the age of 16. Parents of children studying full time up to the age of 19 also qualify. It is currently £15.50 a week for the first child and £10.35 for each other child. You do not have to be the child's parent to obtain it and it is not affected by income or savings. You can claim as soon as your child is born or comes to live with you.

Childcare Tax Credit

This is a relatively new payment which benefits low-paid parents and allows them to work at the same time. Low-paid working parents, often lone mothers, qualify for a childcare tax credit to help pay for childcare while they work. You can claim up to 70 per cent of the cost of a childminder, nursery, out-of-hours clubs on school premises and childcare schemes run on crown property such as some hospitals. The maximum you can claim for childcare is £100 for one child and £150 for two or more children.

Child Maintenance

You may be entitled to Child Maintenance from the other parent of your child if you live apart. It is in addition to any other income you may have, provided you do not get a social security benefit (apart from child benefit). If your children spend part of the time with you and part of the time with the other parent, the child maintenance will be shared. This is provided that the children spend at least 104 nights a year with the other parent (an average of two nights a week).

The amount you receive through Child Maintenance varies according to a formula agreed by Parliament. The basic weekly benefit for a new-born child is around £71, assuming Child Benefit of £15.50. The other parent is usually not expected to pay more than thirty per cent of his net income in child maintenance. You can check your entitlement by dialling the national enquiry line for Child Maintenance (0845 7133 133).

If your partner does not pay at all, you may ask the Child Support Agency to make him do so. Payments can be deducted directly from wages or salary, up to forty per cent of income – the extra ten per cent is a punishment for failing to pay. However, as the case of Carole shows, this can be a long struggle.

When the child maintenance payments stop: Carole had worked as a secretary in central London for five years when she became pregnant. She was not married. The father of her daughter, Chloe, abandoned her as soon as the child was born. He refused to pay any maintenance. He even denied that Chloe was his.

Carole earns £18,000 a year. But she has a mortgage on a house in Essex and until her daughter started school, she had to pay £92 a week to a childminder. She also pays hefty commuting fares. She leaves home before eight and returns at 6.45pm. Once her bills are paid, her take-home pay is small. However, because her gross income seems relatively high, she has had little co-operation from the Child Support Agency.

'They seem to prioritise mothers who are on income support becauses it saves the State money. It took three years to get money and then the father stopped paying after nine months. I was not even warned that he had stopped.'

When Chloe's father cut his maintenance payments, Carole could not keep up with her mortgage and was threatened with repossession by the bank. 'I was so worried about what would happen to us,' she said. 'Luckily a colleague helped me out and talked to the bank and helped arrange financial advice for me. He noticed I was upset and asked me what the matter was.'

Carole has since obtained regular maintenance payments. The money is taken from the father's wages.

If you are a mother on low pay with savings below £8,000, you may be entitled to Income Support, but only if you are working an average of less than 16 hours a week or your partner is working less than 24 hours a week. If you qualify, you are entitled to free milk and vitamins during your pregnancy. Your child will also get free milk and vitamins up to the age of five. You may be able to get extra money if you are buying your home plus some help with other housing costs.

Working Families Tax Credit

The Working Families Tax Credit (WFTC) guarantees a minimum income of £207 a week to low-income families, rising to £214 a week from April 2001. If you (together with your partner if you have one) work 16 hours or more a week and you have one or more children aged under sixteen (or under 19 if still at school), you may be entitled. It is paid to about 1.5 million families including those with slightly above-average incomes.

The aim is to make work more attractive to low-earners caught in the 'poverty trap'. In the past, it paid many mothers to stay on benefit because paying income tax on an earned income left them worse off. In the government's budget in March 2000, it was announced that all lone mothers on benefits will be forced to attend interviews about working once their children reach the age of five. They will be encouraged to work full-time or work part-time without losing benefits. They can also take a £15 a week grant while studying. Mothers will not be forced to return to work. It will still be possible to be a full-time mother on benefits.

Mothers on maternity leave, single or married, will be able to claim WFTC for six months as long as they were working before they gave birth. The benefit will be means-tested and is worth up to £30 a week for the poorest mothers. The wealthier will get nothing.

The main beneficiaries of WFTC are lone parents who work more than 16 hours a week. If you earn less than £17,000 a year, you can qualify for 70 per cent of your weekly childcare bills to a maximum of £100 for one child and £150 for two or more. You are still entitled to child maintenance from an absent father. However, if you earn more, your housing benefit will be withdrawn.

You can be employed or self-employed. The benefit, up to a maximum of £52.30, lasts 26 weeks. If it is renewed, it stays the same even if you earn more or your wages drop. Once your family's net income is more than £90 a week, 55 pence of every excess pound is deducted from the maximum Working Families Tax Credit. In theory, if you have many children, you can qualify for WFTC if you earn as much as £32,000.

There is a Working Families Tax Credit helpline on 0845 609 5000. You can also find out details by using the Department of Social Security website at www.dss.gov.uk.

SureStart Maternity Grant

This is paid to more than 200,000 low-income mothers who meet a basic requirement of health check-ups for young children. It is currently worth £200. From autumn 2000 it is increased to £300.

Social Fund payments

There are Social Fund maternity payments available for low-income mothers. The idea is to help with the cost of equipment for your new baby. You qualify if you or your partner are getting Income Support, income-based Jobseeker's Allowance, Family Credit or Disability Working Allowance. The payment does not have to be paid back and you can claim from eleven weeks before your baby is due until three months after the birth.

If you are adopting, your baby must be under twelve months old and the claim must be within three months of adoption. If your baby is born by surrogacy, you or your partner must have a parental order. Claims must be made within three months of obtaining such an order.

Disability Living Allowance

If you are bringing up a child under 16 who is ill or disabled, you may be able to get Disability Living Allowance or Severe Disablement Allowance for them. To find out if you qualify, telephone your local social security office.

Widowed Mother's Allowance

For widows bringing up children, or expecting their late husband's baby, there is the Widowed Mother's Allowance, which is available if you are not getting Child Benefit. Not all children count for the Widowed Mother's Allowance, so you must check with your social security office first.

6: TELLING YOUR BOSS AND COLLEAGUES

Only when you are clear how you will manage the care of your baby and have a fair idea of what work options are available to you, should you discuss your pregnancy and your plans for your return to work with your employer. You should also be pretty well informed about your rights – you may need them.

Even in these enlightened, job-protected times, pregnancy scares employers. It is inconvenient. It costs them money and raises a whole range of disturbing questions. Who will do your work while you are on maternity leave? Will you return to your job or change your mind? Will you be the same employee when you return? Will you take lots of time off to be with your baby? Your boss needs reassurance that your good news is not bad news for his or her business.

If you are ill-prepared, you risk everything, as one 28-year-old mother-to-be in County Durham discovered in 1998.

Fired because she was pregnant: *Claire lost her job as a legal executive because she was pregnant with her first child. Her bosses, two soliticitor brothers from Darlington, County Durham, fired her the day before she would have been entitled to extended maternity leave and full employment protection.*

It was a devastating blow for Claire. Her £17,000 annual income was vital because her husband Philip's farm at Eppleby in North Yorkshire was in severe financial difficulty. The beef crisis brought about by the spread of mad cow disease had ruined his business. At the age of 28, Claire was the effective breadwinner of the family. They had to borrow money to help pay their mortgage.

An industrial tribunal in Newcastle-upon-Tyne decided that the two solicitor brothers felt they had to get rid of Claire 'because of her pregnancy and everything that went with it', including statutory maternity pay, the right to maternity leave and the right to return to her job when her maternity leave had ended.

They awarded Claire substantial compensation, deciding that she had been unfairly dismissed and was the victim of sexual discrimination.

*She was entitled to 14 weeks' maternity pay and her job back no matter
how long she had been employed. Claire and her husband were forced to
borrow money to pay the mortgage on their home.*

Claire might have avoided her sacking if she had announced her
pregnancy after she had worked for her firm long enough to qualify for
full employment protection. Full protection now comes only after one
year's continuous service. You are only obliged to warn your employer
21 days before the start of your planned maternity leave. In theory,
therefore, even before the new rules came in, Claire could have waited
until she was eight months pregnant before breaking the news to
her bosses.

It is not enough to rely on your rights. In the end, as the example above
shows, an employer may still get rid of you. Claire won compensation
but she lost her job and suffered great financial hardship.

Some bosses are determined to make it difficult for new mothers.
This is very foolish. Their firms, like Claire's employers, are likely to
end up before Industrial Tribunals trying to justify the way they have
behaved. Damages are now unlimited for cases of sexual discrimination
and future recruitment for that firm may be jeopardised if it has
subjected mothers to harsh treatment.

However, you also have a responsibility to your employers. If you
do not state clearly how you expect your baby to affect your capacity
to work, your bosses may feel badly let down. They may honour their
legal duties, but they will write you off as no longer ambitious or
conscientious. Your promotion prospects may be harmed.

Softening the blow

You should have the answers to some crucial questions before they are
asked – who will care for your baby when you return? How many
hours will you really be able to work? How will your baby affect your
ability to travel if your job requires it?

When I was pregnant with my first son I waited until I had had an
amniocentesis test before I told my boss that I was pregnant. I gave him
the good news by inviting him to lunch and telling him that I wanted
to discuss my future. He thought that I was going to announce that I
was leaving or demand promotion and was relieved that a baby was all
I had in mind.

I said that I intended to work as long as possible before the baby was born. I kept my word. My son was born on a Sunday. I worked until the Friday before. Luckily, I was happy and healthy. I had none of the false labours suffered by friends who had spent weeks at home before the birth of their children.

How long you can work will depend on your health, the type of job you do and how far you have to travel to work. There is no need to try to be superhuman because you are pregnant. It is better to be realistic, to minimise the inconvenience your pregnancy will cause by solving as many of the potential problems as you can.

I lived about three miles from my office. This meant that the daily journeys in late pregnancy and early motherhood were not difficult. My husband had already adapted the basement of our home into his office. I added a modem to the computer and a fax machine, which I paid for myself. When I first broached the subject of motherhood with my boss, I told him that I expected to resume working from home two weeks after the baby was born. For the first two weeks, I told him, I would work entirely from home, apart from occasional visits to the office, then I would spend mornings at home and afternoons in the office.

Because I was already a trusted employee, this arrangement – part teleworking and part office working – was a good compromise for everyone. I would often send the first messages of the day via the computer wearing my dressing gown. I could express enough milk for the baby's feeds when I was not there. I got a great deal done between nine and one when I was working at home. If someone from outside the office needed to speak to me urgently during the morning my secretary would tell them that I was on another line and would ring back. She was not lying, I was on another line – at home. She then either telephoned, faxed or sent a computer message asking me to call the person in question. No-one ever guessed that I was expressing milk or feeding my baby while I talked to them.

After lunch, I set off for the office at about 2.20pm and stayed until about 8pm. The office got a very productive ten-hour-day from me when I was contracted to do eight. I had a lovely first six months with my first baby.

The twelve golden rules

Here are the twelve rules of engagement for all first-time mothers:

Rule 1: Do your homework in advance. Before you tell your employer, find out what kind of childcare is available in your price range. Work out if you can cover your old working hours. Assess how many hours you would ideally like to work.

Rule 2: Tell your boss first. You can always ask him or her to keep it quiet initially but say that you want him or her to know early because you are committed to returning to work and want him or her to know this. The law insists that you tell your employer that you are pregnant at least 21 days before you plan to start your maternity leave. However, for most firms, this is very short notice, particularly if you are entitled to more than the basic 18 weeks of maternity pay.

Rule 3: Offer to get all your work up to date when you go on maternity leave and prepare a full checklist for whoever will do your job in your absence. Where possible, spend time making sure that your deputy is properly prepared.

Rule 4: Propose a plan for your return. Your employer is likely to be more flexible about your eventual working week if you are willing to keep in touch during your early weeks and months of motherhood. The idea that panics a boss most is the idea of your losing touch with your job when you start your leave.

Rule 5: Put your plan in writing and get your boss to agree to it in writing. He or she may agree something in principle before you have your baby, but then have second thoughts later on. Without an agreement in writing, you may return from your maternity leave to find someone else doing your old job while you are assigned a new task.

*A **change of boss:** This nearly happened to me. When I was having my second baby I had a chat with my boss. He was a father and was very relaxed about everything that I suggested. He was worried that I was expecting too much of myself. He wanted me to wait until the baby was born before I made a firm commitment. I went ahead and put all my* *proposals in writing, adding in caveats about my plans being dependent on my health and that of the baby.*

However, while I was in hospital after the early arrival of the baby, my boss left the company. His replacement was far less family-friendly. Several years later, I saw a note in my personnel file. It said that my new boss had not been happy with my agreement. He felt working from home could set a precedent for other journalists. If I had not had a full note of the original agreement with my old boss in my file, I could have found myself renegotiating within days of giving birth.

Rule 6: For most mothers, full-time work is too much when their babies are small. Find out how many people work part time at your company and what arrangements already exist. Most employers now recognise that they can get better value from a part-time but committed worker than from an over-stretched full-time one. They also know that to refuse part-time work could form the basis for a sex discrimination claim. Under the European Part-Time Work Directive, it will soon be illegal to pay you less per hour because you are a part-timer. You may even be able to negotiate a higher rate of pay if you are willing to be 'at the end of the phone' on your day or days off to deal with problems.

The teacher who did not plan for stress: *Wilma thought she could remain in her job full-time after the birth of her son, Eddie. She was a special needs teacher at the Barclay School in Stevenage, Hertfordshire, with ambitions to become a deputy head teacher. But within a few weeks, she was forced to change her mind. The combination of childcare and her job proved too demanding and she opted to work part time.*

She was in her early thirties when she became pregnant. She had taken a masters degree and thought she could cope with bringing up a child and holding down a full-time job. She returned to work when her son was seven months old, but within thirteen weeks, she realised she was out of her depth.

'The stress was too much,' she said. 'I lost a stone in three weeks.' Luckily, her husband David had a full-time job as a teacher and her employer was sympathetic to her request to go part time. She continued with the arrangement when her second son, Ben, was born five years later. She has now gradually built up her work to four-and-a-half days a week.

'I was very lucky that I was in a profession where I could go part time,' she said. 'I did a lot of soul-searching when I went back to work, but I feel in the end I did the right thing.'

Rule 7: Find out what is included in the maternity benefit package your company offers. Check with other mothers if they had any problems with the package. Some companies, for example, require an employee to return for at least six months after having the baby or expect all or part of the maternity benefit to be refunded. This is largely intended to stop mothers moving to other companies after receiving generous maternity benefit from their old employers.

Rule 8: Be flexible and willing. The more flexible you are, the more your boss is likely to be relaxed about the change that is about to befall you.

Rule 9: Make it clear that you have done your research into childcare and have arrangements lined up, or at least that you know what is available near your home or your work.

Rule 10: Do not be defensive. Be organised and confident in describing how your job will accommodate your baby. You have the right to have a baby. If your boss is less than helpful he could end up paying you substantial compensation. Employers should not stand in the way of reasonable requests made to help a mother to look after her family.

Rule 11: Try to organise your antenatal examinations and classes at times that fit in with your work. I used to go to my GP's surgery at 8am – the opening time. My hairdresser Nicky has managed to fit in her antenatal hospital appointments on her days off. You are legally entitled to take time off work to attend antenatal appointments, but it is diplomatic to make these convenient to your employer.

Rule 12: Be sympathetic to non-parents. Not all are childless by choice. Some will be jealous. Others will be irritated that they will have to cover for you when you are on maternity leave. If you are able to offer assistance by working a shift for a colleague or by volunteering for bank holiday cover in your early pregnancy, your fellow workers are less likely to mind covering for you when you are away.

Of course, all rules are made to be broken. The above are guidelines to get you to think early about how you are going to manage and to encourage you to think about how your pregnancy and time away from work will affect others.

Mother of twins who won the popularity vote: Jane worked as a picture researcher in central London when she became pregnant with twins. She let her employer know about her pregnancy very early because she suffered badly from morning sickness.

'I had no choice,' she said. 'I was only ten weeks pregnant but I was very ill and I had to tell Human Resources that I was expecting a baby. I then discovered it was twins. They were very understanding. I did not discuss how the babies would affect my work because I could not think that far ahead. It was only during my maternity leave that I fixed an appointment to discuss changing to a four-day week.'

Jane found out that her company gave £250 in John Lewis or Marks and Spencer vouchers for women employees who took maternity leave. She bought a tumble dryer. She worked until six weeks before her twin daughters Sophie and Kate were born.

'I did not get much hostility from the others at work. Everyone knew I was having twins because I was so big. I was getting further and further away from my computer terminal until I could hardly reach the keyboard. It was a big joke. I worked until six weeks before the birth.'

Six weeks before her maternity leave ended, Jane found out about nurseries near her home and her work and chose one next to the mainline station in central London where she and her husband Graham arrive every day from the north London suburbs. She arranged to work a four-day week.

It pays to ask other working mothers in your organisation about their experiences of pregnancy and maternity leave, so that you can judge your employers' attitudes. Clearly, Jane judged her company correctly. It was one which was relaxed about flexible working because it recognised the long-term benefits, particularly the savings on recruitment and retraining.

If, however, the culture in your organisation is hostile towards working mothers (and fathers who put their families on an equal footing with their jobs), there is only one course of action – you must prepare for the worst and hope that you are proved wrong.

The victim of macho culture: Lydia, from Guildford in Surrey, knew she was in a hostile environment. Only 44 of the 262 employees at the computer software company where she worked were female. She became pregnant in her late thirties while working as a business consultant for the company. She took maternity leave, but was made redundant before she could return to work.

She won more than £60,000 compensation in an out-of-court settlement after an industrial tribunal found her firm, Origin UK, guilty of sexual discrimination and unfair dismissal. She had been at the firm for five years and was earning £28,000 a year. She had a company car and other benefits. She said she was far better qualified than her male counterparts and had just completed an MBA degree.

Hardly had her daughter Eloise been born than she received a letter from her boss ordering her to return her company car. She was mystified. It had been agreed that she would keep it while on maternity leave.

The company made her and eleven of her colleagues redundant but did not tell her until three days later.

'I had not had a real chance to start enjoying motherhood before the harassment started,' she said. 'They were trying to make savings and they thought they could force me out.'

The firm agreed that she had been unfairly dismissed because she had had no warning, had not been consulted and had not been able to appeal. But it claimed there was no sexual discrimination because it had treated eleven other employees equally badly, a justification described by the tribunal chairman as 'a sort of insanity defence'.

The fight for compensation was long and hard. It took Lydia eighteen months to bring her case before a tribunal. She conducted her own case. Her husband Derek, a research chemist, had been planning a career break and was going to do a part-time master's degree to allow Lydia return to work. Now he found himself looking after the baby while she worked on the files to support her case for unfair dismissal.

'It was tremendously time-consuming,' she said. 'I was going home, spending a bit of time with Eloise and then leaving Derek to look after her while I looked at all the files.'

She said money was not the issue. 'I just felt that this treatment should not be tolerated. The birth had been very difficult and I was just starting to recover when I was told to return the car. When the letter came, I was extremely angry. I was treated shabbily and employers should learn they cannot do this to women in a vulnerable position.'

Lydia now has a job as a part-time tutor.

7: THE PREGNANT PAUSE

Pregnancy at work is potentially comic. There is no use in beating about the bush. If you look like an egg and you can't stay awake, your efforts to look cool and professional are, sooner or later, bound to come a cropper.

For Karen, the conference room of her London company was her undoing. It was usually empty at lunchtimes. Karen worked as middle-ranking employee in one of the offices nearby. Pregnant with her first child, she found work during the early months exhausting. She needed to take a nap for an hour every lunchtime. She had suffered several miscarriages and was determined not to put her baby at risk.

Most days, she made the long walk to the company medical room and slept on a proper bed. The nurse would wake her when it was time to return to work. She passed the conference room each day on her journey. Invariably, it was empty. One day, she thought it would be easier to push three chairs together in the conference room and sleep there rather than make the trek down two flights of stairs and along the road into the main company building. She pushed the chairs together and lay down. They made a surprisingly comfortable bed. She was so tired, she fell asleep in a moment. After an hour, she woke, refreshed. She returned to her desk for the afternoon's work.

Soon she was using the conference room most lunchtimes until one day she overslept. She woke to find herself surrounded by grey suits about to start a business meeting. They had not noticed her as they came in. She raised herself up, apologised and left the room with considerable embarrassment.

Male colleagues are often embarrassed by pregnancy. They find it difficult to see you as a co-worker when you are simultaneously a human being about to give birth. The two do not seem compatible. You should, after all, play only one role at once. To parade your 'medical condition' when you should be getting on with business is, well... impolite. If you were a diabetic would you insist on injecting insulin during business meetings in full view of your colleagues? Why couldn't you have your pregnancy out of working hours or during your breaks?

Many men also mistakenly think that going to work puts you at more risk than staying at home. This is illogical. A senior company executive was horrified to see me at a press conference in central London when I was seven months pregnant. It was too much of a strain, he said. Yet he freely admitted that his own stay-at-home wife had done all the supermarket shopping when she was seven months pregnant. I pointed out that all that lifting and bending and stretching was harder work than listening to a financial presentation and making notes. It was also true that in central London I was probably closer to a hospital than his wife had been while she loaded her trolley in Sainsbury's.

I have also seen the uncomfortable look on the face of the chief executive of a big national company when he spotted my 'bump' at the end of a business meeting. With Rory, my first child, I was very healthy and the bump was reasonably small. I was able to work as a financial journalist until 8pm on the Friday night before he was born. He arrived on Sunday. In that final week I went for a business lunch at the Savoy Hotel in central London.

I arrived early and sat down at the table reading the menu until the chief executive arrived. Then we got down to business talking about developments in the City. I did not think to discuss my pregnancy as I intended to get back to work quickly.

At the end of the meal I stood up to shake his hand. He looked down. He turned pale and said: 'I didn't know you were pregnant. I would never have expected you to come here if I had known. When is the baby due?' I replied: 'Yesterday.' He appeared to be in more need of medical attention than I was.

He sent a large bouquet when my baby finally did arrive.

Maternity clothes

Clothes are a problem for any working mother-to-be who has to look smart for work. Business suits, especially, are not designed to expand as your body inflates. There is no easy answer to this except to adopt a new style – one which does away with waists. Long dark jackets and loose shirts or sweaters can disguise a great deal if they are worn as if you mean it.

Look in the fashion magazines and choose loose styles which look good on skinny models, but which also have the capacity to expand. Catalogues which specialise in fashions for 'larger' women often have garments designed to flatter your waist. If they come with trousers or skirts with waists, buy the bottoms two sizes too big and use safety pins to keep them in place while you are thin, letting them out gradually as you grow larger.

Women who would normally be happy to spend several hundred pounds on work outfits are reluctant to do so for the final weeks of a pregnancy. If they have to buy an evening dress for two or three functions, they resent it even more.

I benefited from borrowing clothes from a neighbour who had just had a baby. She was a little taller than me but with flowing garments this was not a problem. I bought a couple of loose shirts and one evening dress. The dress went on to be borrowed by two other women at work and then to be used for my second pregnancy.

How to annoy your colleagues

Antenatal classes and hospital appointments are among the biggest causes of resentment among your workmates. You have a right to attend them during working hours (see page 98). But if you are in the middle of an important project and you announce that you have to leave for a spot of deep-breathing and bonding with your fellow mothers-to-be, your colleagues might feel betrayed.

There are diplomatic ways round this. If you plan your appointments around your work, you may get away without your colleagues even noticing your absence. You can share your antenatal appointments between your GP and the hospital. Many GPs offer appointments before or after working hours. What is more, they see you within the hour. You will still need to attend the hospital antenatal clinics, however, and suffer their interminable delays. Many NHS hospitals tend to book all their antenatal appointments for 9am and 2pm. Expectant mothers turn up at the same time and have to wait in line for hours. If you can keep these endurance sessions down to once a month or less, your colleagues may not resent your absence. If you are taking a whole morning off once a week, you are bound to cause annoyance.

If you work irregular patterns or always have Mondays off it might be possible to fit in your antenatal appointments then. This is above and beyond the call of duty. You are legally entitled to attend antenatal appointments during work time. Therefore you must make sure that your line manager and colleagues know what you have done. If you do not win brownie points for your unselfishness, what is the point of it all?

Tiredness is a real problem for any mother-to-be and another cause of annoyance to colleagues who need you to be awake. At work you cannot hide. A nap at home goes unnoticed. A nap during the working day is taboo. After all, you are being paid the same as non-pregnant colleagues who are wide awake. Until we reach the point when pregnant women are allowed 'sleep breaks', the only reasonable course of action is to fight your tiredness and hope you are not caught out.

I was literally caught napping. About 20 weeks into my first pregnancy I had to attend the annual Building Societies Association conference in Bournemouth. I arrived at the hotel mid-afternoon and decided to have a little sleep because the speeches at the evening function would go on until late. I asked for a wake-up call at 6.30pm to make sure that I got to the reception on time. When it came the hotel operator said: 'This is your wake-up call and your office has been trying to get hold of you for the last 90 minutes.'

A big story had broken in the late afternoon. With only two hours before the newspaper deadline, my City Editor wanted me to talk to the key people involved. Where was I? The hotel had insisted that I could not be disturbed. It took quite a bit of living down.

One former colleague used to amuse us all with her use of bananas to overcome tiredness at work during her pregnancy. Every day she would arrive at her desk with vast quantities of bananas which she nibbled through the day. They were far better for her than biscuits or chocolate. We admired her planning skills. You have to think ahead to have fruit at your desk in the quantities needed to give you the equivalent energy of sugary snacks.

Careless talk costs friends

Another source of annoyance to non-pregnant colleagues is constant pregnancy prattle and baby-talk. This cannot be overstated. Your pregnancy seems such an important thing to you that it is easy to assume that everyone else is equally thrilled. They are not. They are at work to get on with their jobs. Think of how annoyed you are when colleagues spend too much time talking on the phone to their boyfriends or girlfriends instead of working. They may be in love, but if their emotional state makes them a pain to work with, you are likely to resent them rather than be thrilled for their good fortune.

The same applies to pregnancy. Do not keep talking about it, unless a colleague initiates the subject. Even then, try to keep your mind on the main task – your job. One pregnant colleague of mine became so obsessed by her condition that she congratulated an overweight secretary on her 'good news'. The overweight secretary was not pregnant at the time. She was understandably upset and joined Weight Watchers shortly afterwards.

Many of your colleagues – especially young single women – will be hostile to your pregnancy because they resent the inconvenience it will cause them. An insight into this was given on a recent BBC *Panorama* programme in which a 26-year-old business analyst called Helen Patterson described her feelings.

Ban the mum: *'People who have children too often phone up and say "I can't come in today because little Tommy's feeling sick, I can't do this because my childminder's poorly",' she said. 'They let you down at the last minute whereas I couldn't ring my boss today and say I don't really feel like work today, I can't come in, it's not acceptable.*

'I think having a child wouldn't fulfil me and it would prevent me from having the career that I would like to choose. How many managing directors do you know who are females? How many managing directors are women returners? It just doesn't happen.

'I see working mothers as people who are trying to juggle too many balls and at some point they're going to drop the lot. The pressure of their workload will fall to me. They can probably hold down a job if they were working part time in a supermarket or library or whatever but I don't think they can accept the high pressure responsibility of high-powered jobs.

'I feel new laws on part-time work would not be welcomed by employers and I wouldn't be as appealing to them. It's just hassle for them and they would wrongly assume that at some point I'm going to want those rights and I'm going to be contacting personnel and I'm going to want time off and legally they would have to give it to me. It would hinder myself and people like me. I'm being realistic. If some women choose to have children, then they must expect their lifestyle's going to change, they can't have it all.'

This hostility is no laughing matter. It reflects the male culture of many British businesses. Helen is voicing her genuine insecurity about being sidelined. She works in an investment bank in the City of London, the kind of institution which is very intolerant of working mothers and rarely promotes them to positions of high responsibility. She has identified working mothers as a threat because she sees them being regarded as non-ambitious. She is afraid she will be tarred with the same brush.

In more family-friendly working environments, Helen would see that working mothers thrive and do rise to the top. However, mothers must reassure their colleagues that they have organised their pregnancies and childcare well in advance, so that it will be pretty much business as usual when they return.

You must be diplomatic. Insisting that everyone stops smoking to protect your unborn child is likely to raise many hackles. But, once again, there are soft solutions. In my office, smoking was the norm until a secretary confided in her boss that she was pregnant and was worried about the effects of passive smoking. Her boss was sympathetic and organised a ballot among the staff. He said the risk of passive smoking was now proven and the company had a duty to consult staff about whether they wanted smoking banned. The vote for clean air was won and the secretary's victory has made the office a healthier place for any pregnant woman.

Antenatal classes

The time before your baby is born is also theoretically when you can prepare yourself physically for the birth itself. If my friends' and my own experience is anything to go by, this is very much over-rated. If you were unfit before you got pregnant and you have done little by way of exercise since, no amount of heavy breathing and pelvic thrusting is going to make you an Olympic-class mother in the few weeks between stopping work and giving birth. Besides, unless you plan to give birth African-style in a field, you will have your own personal trainer on hand when you finally go into labour. That is what midwives are for.

One of the big surprises about your first pregnancy is that it can make you political. Join any antenatal class and you will find yourself dealing with competing ideologies about how you should conduct yourself before, during and after giving birth.

Should your husband or partner accompany you to antenatal classes? Should he learn deep-breathing techniques in sympathy with you? Should you insist on a home birth? A 'natural' birth? Should your partner be there? What is your attitude to caesareans or epidural injections? Should you breastfeed? What do you plan to do when your baby cries?

Some antenatal classes, especially those provided by your local health authority, try to be less political than others. Yet you cannot avoid ideology because there are genuinely so many choices you must make. Take the home-versus-hospital debate, for instance. Many health authorities prefer you to have your baby in hospital for medical reasons. If there are complications, the chances of a successful medical intervention are far greater if you are in hospital. On the other hand, the rising number of caesarian births in hospitals has a lot to do with the convenience to medical staff. Predicting the precise moment of birth may be more important than the health of the mother or her baby. In Scotland, the home-versus-hospital debate also includes the treatment of fathers. Many are effectively excluded from being present at the birth of their children because they cannot afford the cost of travelling to distant district hospitals.

The largest and best-known childbirth charity, the National Childbirth Trust (NCT) has 380 branches across the UK with 40,000 members. It also has its own website (www.nct-online.org) with details of its many publications. It campaigns for improvements in midwife support, the right to home birth and the increased use of breastfeeding, among other issues.

If you are a working mother, it can seem a waste of time to attend antenatal classes when there are countless books on the subject of pregnancy, labour, healthy eating, breastfeeding and so on. Many of the classes are in the afternoon and early evening and workers can find it hard to attend.

But the classes offer something you cannot find in books – a network of local mothers whose experiences you can draw on, and a support system in times of need. Even if you do not attend a class yourself, it is worth making friends with a mother-to-be who does. She can introduce you to other mothers whose children will be roughly the same age as your own. A nanny shared between two households is often as cheap as a childminder and much more convenient.

The chances are that there will be many other working mothers at your antenatal or post-natal classes. Their advice can be invaluable. For example, I learned to express milk into a bottle as soon as possible after the birth. My baby could then be fed by my husband as well as by me. Leave it until the baby is six months old and the baby will have much more difficulty in adjusting to a bottle. This also makes other forms of childcare more difficult if you want to return to work early.

What the antenatal classes can teach you are the rules of diet and how to avoid habits such as smoking and drinking which can harm your baby. They are also the best chance you will have to create your own support group of other mothers. There is almost bound to be someone in your antenatal class or at the clinic whom you find sympathetic. A mother with a child roughly the same age as yours is a great potential ally. You can learn from her mistakes (and vice-versa). You may even be able to share childcare if you live near each other or if her employer's premises are near your workplace.

The urge to spend

First-time mothers often go over the top in their preparations, spending weeks decorating the baby's room, buying every baby manual in sight, piling up huge quantities of equipment and clothing.

Every second-time mother wonders why any first-time mother would bother to do half these things. Do you really need an elaborate nursery with 'stimulating' animal pattern wallpaper and pictures on the ceiling? All the baby can see are the toys dangling immediately above the cot. Many parents prefer to have their babies sleeping with them in their own bedroom for the first few months, anyway. They want to be able to hear if the baby is distressed. They do not want to have to go wandering in the dark in the middle of the night to another room.

How many clothes can a baby wear? Isn't dressing up in miniature designer suits the last thing a muling, puking infant needs? For months, all he or she will be doing is lying, crying, burping, puking and (eventually) rolling. All your baby needs is a stretchy, washable all-in-one jump suit. Even in mid-winter there is no point in buying full Olympic class ski-wear. The little mite cannot even walk. A carry cot is built for insulation. Second babies are usually far more sensibly dressed than their older siblings because their mothers buy on a 'need-to-wear' basis.

As for toys, small babies need so few of them that it is hardly worth bothering going to a shop to look. Your friends and relations will buy dozens of them, whether you want them or not, and your baby will always choose the most unsuitable one as its favourite, or ignore them all and play with a wooden spoon instead.

Leaving party

If no-one at your workplace offers, organise a 'baby shower', a party to celebrate your coming event. Have a little leaving party in a local pub or restaurant for your colleagues to thank them for all their help and to mark this important rite of passage. You may have been off alcohol for months and need to sit down most of the evening, but it is worth it to give everyone the opportunity to wish you well. It also means that if they have had a collection they can give you the gift at your party and get something back for their contribution!

8: PLANNING YOUR RETURN

You have only a few weeks before and after the birth of your baby to decide how you are going to balance work and family life when you return to work. By the time you go back it is too late – unless you have a very sympathetic employer. You are entitled to return to your old job, but only if you do so full time. There is no right to convert your job into part-time employment, though there is a groundswell of opinion in favour of a change in the law.

At present, if you want to go part time, you must bargain with your boss. If you can do this before your baby is born, so much the better. Once you go back full time, it may be harder to switch.

I know many women who worked right up until the birth of their babies. One lawyer working on a big corporate deal even managed to stay in her office through the early stages of labour. But when the contractions were every four minutes, she left the office for the hospital. Even so, someone questioned why she had not finished the final draft of the contract she was working on instead of leaving it to a colleague. Her baby was born two hours after she arrived at the hospital.

The lesson is that in some jobs however much you do, some employers will still want more!

Organising your departure

During the last three months of your pregnancy you must organise your departure so that your colleagues are not left in the lurch. If you dump all your unfinished business on them they will neither forgive nor forget.

It is important to do this early, just in case the birth is premature. If your work is in a mess, the last thing you should do is to leave it behind as a reminder to your colleagues of how disorganised you are. Once your maternity leave starts, you will not be there to answer back or put things right. The impression you want to leave behind is of the useful, considerate, capable colleague whom everyone wants back at her post. There are always those in every organisation who would like to take advantage of your absence. A messy departure will give them all the ammunition they need.

My second child, Gray, came six weeks prematurely, with no warning. No matter how prepared you might be to hand over to your colleagues, such dramatic turns of events are bound to cause chaos. I still had a diary full of business appointments which had to be cancelled by my secretary.

I am sure this caused some annoyance. However, the suddenness, coupled with the medical risk of the emergency caesarian operation, brought out a great deal of generosity, too. The flowers and fruit arrived in such abundance that my side room was nicknamed Kew Gardens by the nurses. The flowers became a problem. When we got to 40 bouquets and all vases on the ward and at home were full, my secretary called a halt. She persuaded the next batch of cancelled appointments that champagne was the thing to send new mothers. Luckily, it worked. When Gray arrived home, my family and friends had something special with which to toast the baby's health.

The premature arrival of my baby meant that I could not get all my work affairs in order. I had to spend hours on the telephone telling my colleagues where they could find things. I even had to have a work meeting in the hospital. A handover is far better done in person than on the telephone. As soon as you are gone, your colleagues will feel free to criticise you for any extra work your departure has caused. If you can manage to sort out nine-tenths of the problems beforehand, going through each item with the colleagues who have to take on your responsibilities, such details are not seen as 'extra work'. They are merely part of the routine.

Choosing your departure date

You have a duty to look after yourself and your unborn baby. If your job is sedentary, you should be able to work longer – possibly as late as a week before the due date – but you must make time to go for regular check-ups to ensure that the baby is not suffering because of your working. There is research evidence to show that the baby grows more when you are resting, either on holiday or at weekends.

Before the Second World War, women had little say about when they would start their maternity leave. In some jobs they were dismissed as soon as their pregnancy became evident. In others, they were forced to start their leave on the date set by their employer and the State.

Now it is largely up to the mother and her medical advisers when the maternity leave begins from the sixth month of pregnancy onwards. Wherever possible, you should decide on a date and stick to it. If you are indecisive before the baby is born, your colleagues will worry that you will become worse once the baby has arrived.

It is reasonable to say to your boss that you intend to work as long as possible up to the birth. If, for example, your baby is due in early August, you might say you expect to start your maternity leave in early July – four weeks beforehand. But make contingency plans if things go wrong. High blood pressure, swollen ankles or the sheer heat of travelling might mean that you are unable to continue working beyond mid-June. As soon as you realise things are going wrong, explain clearly why you have to change your plans.

It may be possible to fulfil your promise to work until July or even longer by operating from home or by combining office and home working. Teleworking is growing rapidly and comparatively little equipment is needed to do most jobs remotely instead of travelling in to an office. Of course, if you are a waitress or checkout assistant you have little choice but to go in to work. However, a surprising number of jobs previously carried out in offices are now done from home.

Budgeting for childcare

If at all possible you should check out the cost and availability of childcare before you go on maternity leave. It is far easier to do so before the baby is born, while you are a free agent. Afterwards, you have to plan every move like a military operation. Also, nurseries and childminders often have waiting lists, sometimes as long as six months. To choose a nanny takes time, too – you should allow at least three months.

Budgeting for childcare is a vital part of your plan to return to work. If you have a partner, you need to work out how much you can afford. You may, for example, decide that the best arrangement is for both of you to work part time. This involves negotiating with your respective employers. If this sounds complicated, it is often simpler than the alternative, both of you juggling work and childcare.

When part-time working makes sense: *Mandy worked in the Elida Fabergé cosmetics factory in Leeds. Her husband Barry was a long-distance lorry driver. When her second child was born, Mandy decided to continue* *working full time. But her childcare co-ordinator Lynn McCarthy advised her against it.*

'If two people are determined to keep on their full-time jobs, it can get too complicated,' said Lynn. 'She wanted the whole of her and her husband's shift pattern covering by some kind of childcare. She needed her night shifts covered and she wanted a childminder to look after them overnight if she was on the 2-10pm shift rather than have them taken home late at night.'

'We worked out that a childminder was going to cost her £500 a month, and on their wages they couldn't afford it. The only affordable way for many couples is for their own family to take on the childcare or for them to do it themselves. In this case she persuaded her sister not to take a job so that she could look after her two children for her. It would probably have been more sensible if she and her husband had gone part time.'

After the birth

The moment you go into labour you are never totally in control of your life again. You are about to become responsible for another human's entire existence. Your hormones dance a jig. It will be years until you sleep soundly again. It is bound to alter your attitude to work.

No matter how much planning you did before the birth, you must be prepared to change your mind. Women who planned to return to work full time sometimes reassess their finances and opt for part-time employment instead. There is no shame in this. We must all do what we think is best for our baby and ourselves. A few new mothers even decide to give up work altogether. This is fine too, if you can afford to do so. If you cannot pay your bills without working, however, the notion of staying at home to bring up baby in relative poverty is not very appealing. No matter how strong your motherly instincts, self-preservation is stronger.

Most of us make compromises. For me, it was to sacrifice a large part of my earnings to pay for first-class childcare. I had a career I did not want to lose. I enjoyed my job. I paid for a live-in nanny and did as much work as I could from home for several months after the birth. It worked for me and my child. Not everyone has such straightforward choices to make, however.

The pre-birth plan that went wrong: *Kate wanted to work part time after the birth of her baby. But circumstances altered and she was forced* *to take a full-time job. She is a single mother aged 29 who has no support from the father of her child.*

She found it impossible to get work in London when she was pregnant. Employers kept turning her down. In desperation, she did work experience for no pay for a large corporation. When her baby was born, the company offered her a full-time job. She felt she could not say no. She started work when her daughter was three months old and managed a five-day week for nine months.

Her finances were tight. She earned £14,000 a year and had to pay out almost £5,000 to a childminder. The cost of commuting was also steep. Towards her daughter's first birthday Kate suffered from depression and was signed off work for about ten weeks. She discussed her condition with the company doctor and decided to return to work part time on Mondays, Tuesdays and Wednesdays. This gave her four days when she could look after her daughter herself.

She saved £50 a week in childminder costs and another £10 in lower commuter fares. But overall, she had a lower income. After a year, when her daughter started playschool at £25 a week, she could barely meet the fees. Luckily, she was offered promotion and more pay. But she had to sacrifice one of her days off. Now she works a four-day week and feels she has at last achieved a balance between her job and her family life.

New physical demands

The shock for many mothers in sedentary jobs is how physically demanding babies are. Carting them around is very hard work. Before a baby, it is possible to go shopping with both hands. After a baby, your hands are almost literally tied.

Life becomes a constant round of carrying, balancing, heaving, pushing, pulling, grunting and groaning. It is not the baby but the paraphernalia to blame. The simplest task, such as going to visit a friend for a few hours, becomes an expedition. Even if you are lucky enough to have a car, you still have the tedium of loading the carseat, the nappy bag, the lotions, the powders, the roll-up changing mat and the toys – and then lugging them from the street to your friend's fifth-floor apartment without the aid of a lift.

If you use public transport, this same baggage becomes even more cumbersome. You can find yourself starring in a bizarre piece of street theatre. Roll up, roll up, see the death-defying mother as she holds a baby under one arm, two bags over her shoulders, her bus pass between her teeth, while, at the same time, ladies and gentlemen, she attempts to fold a lethal spring-loaded buggy with a single swoop of her other arm!

A journey back from the shops using public transport can be even worse, a repeat performance, but this time with even more props and the real danger of dropping eggs or glass bottles onto the pavement.

As your baby gets older and heavier, you also risk back injury. A twenty-pound baby and a ten-pound car seat may not seem too big a deal, until you try heaving their combined weight out of the back seat of a two-door Ford Fiesta. If you were a diagram in a school science book you would probably be labelled 'third-class lever', the kind least efficient at lifting loads. You will certainly feel like a third-class lever. The strain on your lower back will be enormous. I know of several nannies who have been forced to retire with back injuries caused by years of levering plump infants from the back seats of cars.

Second babies

Things become even more physical with a second baby, especially if your first child is still a toddler, dragging at your skirts. With two children in tow, it is as if the earth's gravity has suddenly become stronger.

During a second pregnancy your work colleagues will show little of the sympathy they exhibited the first time around. The novelty will have worn off. You may be feeling exhausted by morning sickness, but this time it will be regarded as your own fault. You have made your bed, metaphorically-speaking, so you must lie on it. Or rather, you must not lie down anywhere. You must pull your weight.

At home, it is quite possible that you will have little extra support either, especially if your partner is working full time. Few fathers insist on doing all the washing and ironing or even the shopping during a second pregnancy. That is still regarded by most men as a woman's responsibility.

Keeping in touch

You are entitled to a maximum of 29 weeks of your extended maternity leave after your baby is born – provided you have worked for your present employer for at least a year at the eleventh week before the baby is due. This is a long time to keep in touch.

Some women drop completely off the work radar the minute their maternity leave begins – a big mistake. Unless you have decided never return to your present job, you must show commitment to it.

Your handover should include putting in place arrangements for keeping you in touch while you are away. Some organisations like BP Amoco have formalised this by making sure all employees on maternity leave or on a career break are kept up to date with news from work (see page 188–9). They encourage parents to network with other parents in the same organisation by attending workshops before, during and after their maternity leave.

'We try to cover the entire range of information which a working mother will need,' says Marion Hansen, the maternity adviser for BP Amoco. 'We have workshops where childcare advisers tell mothers-to-be about the various kinds and costs of childcare and about the formalities of maternity leave. We have workshops dedicated to the problems associated with taking maternity leave and coping with the stress of leaving your job behind. We have workshops on returning to work, balancing home and work and even a New Fathers' workshop.

'When someone goes on maternity leave, we make sure they don't lose touch. We write a newsletter and tell mothers about any meetings or workshops and invite them to attend if they can. We have a comprehensive e-mail system for those who are connected. We let them know if anything is going to affect their job and they can come in and discuss it. Many of the mothers on maternity leave welcome the chance to meet their colleagues from time to time. It helps them feel they still belong.'

You can do the same for yourself. You should ask your friends at work to keep you informed on a regular basis, either by telephone or by meeting them for lunch from time to time. Keeping up with gossip is important. It means you are still thought of as being an employee rather than someone who once used to work there. It means you know if someone is trying to steal your job or if you have been sidelined. It means you know about any shifts in power (which are never announced publicly). Once you have left the office it is much harder to make these arrangements for staying in touch.

It is even worth doing small amounts of work from home to keep your hand in – if your job is suitable. If your work is manual, such as cooking, cleaning or working as an electrician, this is obviously impossible. However, if your work is office-based, it may well be possible to do some teleworking using a computer at home or in a nearby library.

If you are in the sort of job in which you need to be constantly updated on new legislation or corporate changes, ask for this information to be mailed to you at home so that you do not have to spend days swotting up as soon as you start work again.

It is worth planning several visits to your workplace during the last two months of your maternity leave. It is tempting to take your baby with you, but resist that temptation. One visit with the baby is cute, but twice or three times makes you look like a visiting mother not like a worker who is keen on taking up where she left off. You should do 'dry runs' using the childcarer you have chosen to look after your baby, so that you arrive giving out the distinct impression that you cannot wait to get back on track.

Danger signs

Some mothers have returned to work to find that their temporary replacement has become permanent. If this comes as a surprise, the mother herself must share some of the blame. Out of sight is out of mind unless you do something positive to keep your memory alive. It is not enough to rely on your 'right' to return to your old job. A crafty employer can always argue that your 'old job' no longer exists and that you are about to be offered equivalent work. However, that equivalent job is unlikely to be equivalent in every respect.

It is important to see it from your boss's point of view. What if your replacement is absolutely brilliant? It is very difficult to turn away a first-class worker and welcome back someone who may no longer be fully committed to the job. For most of us, the problem does not arise because bosses take a long time to recognise talent.

Replaced by the 'temporary' substitute: The charity Parents at Work cites the case of Folake, who was replaced by her substitute while she was on maternity leave. She was pregnant with her second child. She had a miscarriage and was very depressed. But worse was to come. When she returned to work, she found her employer had restructured the company and appointed her temporary replacement to her old job. She was sidelined with no desk, no telephone, no apparent role. Shortly afterwards she was made redundant. She claims her employers were getting rid of her because

*they thought she would get pregnant again. None of her 13 female
colleagues was made redundant. None of them had children.*

*She fought her employer for wrongful dismissal with the help of the
Equal Opportunities Commission. They settled out of court but not after a
bitter contest. They withdrew their glowing reference issued when she was
made redundant and claimed she had been a bad worker. She could prove
otherwise. She could also prove that they were doctoring documents to be
used in evidence.*

*'You must be prepared for a low-down, nasty fight,' she said. 'Keep
scrupulous records, a diary, notes and copies of all documents. However
angry you get, you need a clear head.'*

Folake's case demonstrates how vital it is to set up a network of
friendly colleagues before you go on maternity leave. The fact that
she did not know about the 'restructuring' of the company until
she returned means she had lost touch. If she suspected before her
maternity leave that her employers were trying to get rid of her, she
should have taken pre-emptive action. She should have drafted a plan
for her return to work and presented it in writing to her boss. She
should have obtained written agreement to it.

The fact that her miscarriage and depression would have prevented
the implementation of this plan is not relevant. She would have given
her employers no option but to think earlier about her future role and
make firm commitments to her before she went away.

Your exploratory visits to work should tell you if your job is in danger.
If, before your maternity leave started, you did not obtain a written
agreement spelling out how and when you would return to work (see page
111), now is the time to take remedial action. The first thing to remember
is that you have rights. You are entitled to return to the same job on the
same terms and conditions (see page 102). You should present your boss
with your return-to-work plan and get him or her to sign it.

If you gain the distinct impression that you are no longer welcome
in your old job, make things difficult. Write down a plan for your return
to work. Make it sound positive and constructive, the kind of plan that
would impress an industrial tribunal that you are a good worker willing
to put yourself out. Make sure that it spells out the current rules and
regulations so that your employer knows that there will be compensation
to pay if you do not get your statutory entitlements (see page 102).
Most situations are not lost until new appointments have been made.

If you have not been replaced, it is easier for your employer to reinstate you than to risk an industrial tribunal.

It is, of course, still possible for a bad employer to cheat on any agreement you have made, as a nurse from Liverpool recently discovered.

The 'reduced hours' job that did not happen: Denise worked as a nurse at a nursing home in Liverpool, earning £17,000 a year. She took maternity leave to have her fourth child and got her boss to agree to reduced working hours when she returned. She was not to work weekends or cover 12-hour shifts.

But when she returned, she was put under pressure several times to work extra hours. Finally, she was asked to work a 12-hour shift to cover for a nurse who was going on leave. She resigned and took the nursing home to an industrial tribunal.

She was awarded £4,100 compensation. The tribunal chairman said that the company had been happy at first to have Denise back on her terms and there was a 'concluded agreement' to this fact. The continual undermining of this was a 'breach of trust and confidence.'

Denise stuck to her guns, even when her boss offered her a shorter shift pattern for less pay. She was entitled to the conditions her employer had agreed. However, her level of her compensation was small compared with the loss of earnings she inevitably suffered through losing her job. She was lucky to be in a profession in relatively high demand so that she could find alternative work.

The end of maternity leave

When your maternity leave runs out, you must return to work at once. Even a day's delay will invalidate your statutory rights. However, if you are ill, you have four weeks' leeway, provided you have completed two years' continuous employment and you can provide a medical certificate from your GP or another doctor.

The clerk who was sacked for being ill: Janet from Durham won a case in 1998 against her former employer, Kwik Save Stores, when she was unfairly dismissed from her job as a clerk for failing to return to work on the first day after her maternity leave.

She returned to her employer's premises to deliver a sick note, but, because she was not able to work, her employer ended her contract of employment. The Court of Appeal said her employers had 'taken advantage of a temporary illness of a female employee to deny her the statutory right to return to work.'

Janet was brave and persistent. She took the trouble to find out what her rights were and saw it through. The law was absolutely clear on this point. Her employers either took bad legal advice or were vindictive.

9: LONE MOTHERS

Looking after a baby or small child is daunting for any parent. If you are on your own, you need to make sure that you have some sort of support system. If you do not have family nearby you have to strengthen ties with other parents.

You might be able to do them favours by babysitting, getting in some practice before your baby is born, taking their child out in its buggy or calling at the shops for them when you do your weekly shop. It is surprising to non-parents how grateful parents can be when someone gives them a hand.

If none of your friends, workmates or neighbours have children or live close enough for you to build a reciprocal relationship, then you should be able to meet people a few pages ahead of you in the childcare book when you go to antenatal clinics and classes. Three months is a long time in the childrearing stakes. You can learn lots and gain confidence from spending time with another mother.

If the relationship develops you can gain more than confidence. You might be able to share childcare or buy clothes or toys cheaply from someone whose child is a little bit older.

Many mothers find childcare is their way back into paid employment. Becoming a childminder can allow you to look after your own child and be paid for looking after those of one or more other families. Many more mothers make informal arrangements so that they look after the other mother's child or children when she is at work and vice versa. These unpaid arrangements make sound economic sense so long as you are confident that the other parent will look after your child as well as you would yourself. You also need to keep a tally of the hours to ensure that one of you does not take advantage of the other.

Such relationships do not always happen naturally. The British tend to stand back and wait for someone else to make the moves. Lone parents can be very lonely if they do not force the pace.

Networking

Young nannies show what can be done. Many of them are away from home for the first time and often on their own in big cities. Every single one of my nannies soon built a network of nanny friends so that they could share the burden of some of the childcare by meeting together at the playground or having a coffee whilst the children played. They would stand in for each other when babysitting was needed or when one was ill.

If you are working, you cannot put all your effort into such networking. But you can make your time off count.

When my children were young we used to go swimming with other parents and children every Sunday morning. Several members of the group met through National Childbirth Trust antenatal classes and introduced their own friends with young children into the circle. After swimming we would stop off at one parent's house to have breakfast and read the papers. It was exhausting looking after babies and toddlers in the pool and getting them back into their clothes. Those croissants and cups of coffee were very welcome. But there was a bonus in getting together – we all noticed that four or five children played better together than the children of one family. We had an hour or so of peace!

The single mothers who combined resources: Carole lives in Essex and works as a secretary in London. She is a single mother with no family nearby to help with childcare. Five months after her daughter Chloe was born she found a childminder near home and went back to work. She became very dependent on the childminder, even arranging her annual holidays to coincide with hers.

'I didn't have anyone else to call on,' she said. 'When there was the Christmas office party at a West End club I paid her to look after Chloe for the evening.'

It was only when Chloe started school that Carole found support from another single mother, Jackie, whose daughter was in the same class as Chloe.

'It's great finding someone in the same boat as you are. We help each other a lot. We go on outings together to various places and on shopping trips,' said Carole. 'It makes a big difference to Chloe because she's got a playmate. Jackie's also helped me out by looking after Chloe while I got on with decorating my house at weekends. It's brilliant. I don't have to worry about Chloe knocking over paint pots or hurting herself while I'm busy.

'I'll help Jackie out the same way to give her a break. I'm on a pretty tight budget because of my mortgage so I might as well make use of what I've got. My house has a small garden and it's great for the kids. In many ways it's less trouble looking after two children who play together than having to entertain one by herself.'

There are all sorts of places where you can go to meet mothers in similar circumstances who may be able to swap childcare or may even be willing to share the rent on a house big enough for two families. If you already have a house and you are on a low income you might improve your financial circumstances by allowing another mother and child to stay with you.

There are baby and toddler swimming classes at most pools, toddler gym lessons and many organisations for lone parents to get together. They could improve your support system, your finances and your ability to cope if you meet another mother you can share with in some way.

Enlisting your family

One obvious solution to childcare is the most traditional – your extended family. If this is coupled with part-time work, you can avoid the problem of 'imposing' on your family's goodwill as well.

The mother who moved 400 miles to be with mum (senior): Jean was in her early thirties when her marriage went sour. Her son David was three. She was working part time for British Telecom in Reading. She says her husband showed no interest in their son. To make matters worse, David was unhappy with his childminder.

'He was always crying. He didn't settle. That was why I only worked two-and-a-half days a week.'

Jean felt isolated even though she was married. She decided to cut her losses and move back to her home town of Hamilton near Glasgow. She found a clerical job with South Lanarkshire Council. It was not well-paid – £6,500 a year – and she could not afford professional childcare.

'I felt it was better for David to have family contact. I did not know who to trust with my child. I knew a childminder across the street who took children from 7am to 6pm, but I felt he would be better off with my mum.'

When David started school, his mother walked him there every day and grandmother would pick him up in the afternoons. Now, at the age of eleven, he can walk to school himself. Jean's mother sometimes has help from her two other daughters who both live nearby in the Udston area of Hamilton.

'I would like to do some work from home, and two-and-a-half days at the office. It would make the childcare easier especially during the summer holidays. My main problem is in-service days for training. At least we have flexitime so I can take a half day off if I want to and make it up later.'

Gingerbread – campaigning for lone parents

The charity Gingerbread is Britain's leading national organisation providing information, support and advice for lone parents and their children. It has local support groups for lone parents all over England and Wales with similar but separate organisations in Scotland and Northern Ireland.

Its policy statement reads as follows: 'Gingerbread has a basic belief; lone parents who are confident, supported and feel good about themselves make better parents than those who are lonely, unhappy and feel a victim of circumstance. We see our work as preventative, seeking to help families deal with their problems rather than leaving them until more costly intervention is needed. The aim is to help lone parents give their children a happy and secure childhood.'

There is an advice line offering expert advice on social security, employment and legal matters. Gingerbread's local support groups provide meeting places for lone parents and their children and try to foster friendship among lone parents who find themselves in similar situations. They are excellent places to find soulmates who might share childcare with you if you can both organise part-time jobs which will dovetail with each other. If you have access to the Internet you can find the nearest support group to you. The website address is: www.gingerbread.org.uk. You can also ask your local library for information and for the number of the advice helpline.

Becoming a childminder

For many single mothers, childminding is an excellent way of earning a living until your own children are at school – provided you have premises suitable for looking after other people's children.

You have to register with your local authority who will inspect your home and advise you how to bring it up to the required standard. There are strict rules about how many children you can look after, including your own – no more than three under the age of five and three children aged between five and eight, including your own children. Each local social services department has different guidelines about the maximum numbers of children over eight, so you must check the rules for your area.

Your home will have to be adapted to make it 'fit premises' for caring for other people's children. Garden ponds, for example, usually have to be filled in or covered. Kitchens have to have extra safety devices. You will need to take out insurance in case of accidents.

The National Childminding Association, a registered charity whose website address is www.ncma.org.uk (use your local library to get in touch), has devised an inexpensive policy indemnifying you for £2 million liability in case a child is accidentally killed or injured while in your care.

The price you can charge varies by area. In central London, childminders charge around £25 per child per day. In other areas it can be as low as £10 per child. Assuming you have two young children of your own and you are looking after four other children, your target income would vary between £200 and £500 a week, depending on the catchment area you serve. If you have room, you can earn more by looking after children over the age of eight before and after school for those parents who have difficulty getting to work and delivering and collecting their children. You would be self-employed and pay your own tax and National Insurance.

Working from home and looking after her daughter: *Jane, from Grantham in Lincolnshire, was 22 when her first daughter Samantha was born. She was working for low wages in an office job for East Midlands Electricity. After her maternity leave she decided to give up her job and become a childminder.*

She said: 'I was living with my mum and dad in a council house. It's got quite a big garden. I looked after two children on a regular basis, a brother and sister aged two and four. I charged £2 an hour. I also had two or three older children most afternoons. I'd pick them up from school and look after them until their mums came home from work.

'I was taking in more than £250 most weeks. I earned more money staying at home as a childminder than I would if I had gone back to work

and employed someone to look after Samantha. It was great being able to combine a job with looking after my daughter. I think she gained from it, too, because she always had someone to play with. I stayed at home until she was four and started school.'

You can go on a training course through the National Childminding Association which can lead to NVQ level 3 in Early Years Care and Education. You could then move on to other jobs within the childcare sphere.

10: SECOND (OR THIRD) TIME AROUND

The more children you have, the harder it is to keep working. When the government conducted a survey in 1994 it found that two thirds of women with one child had jobs. Fewer than half the women who had three or more children were in work.

The main reason is money. Two children at a nursery or with a childminder cost twice as much as one. With three children, your bills triple, but your pay packet does not go up accordingly.

For mothers with two or three children, school is another big obstacle to full-time employment. With a few honourable exceptions, school hours are almost designed to be as inconvenient as possible for work. They start too late and they finish too early. The school holidays – three months of them a year – are hopelessly over-extended.

The chances are that not all of your children will be of school age. This is the worst of all possible worlds. You then have at least two trips to make before you start work – one to the childminder or nursery and a second to the school. Then you have to arrange for the school-age child to be collected and cared for until you finish work. 'School hours' schemes such as the one run for the employees of Watford Council in Hertfordshire solve the problem.

Switching to part-time work

That is why so many working mothers go part-time when their second child is born. This makes perfect sense. It enables you to maximise your income and have more time with your children while paying less for childcare.

You need to sell the idea of switching to part-time work to your employer. In Chapter 4, you can read in detail how to set about this. If you are persuasive, you can keep the best parts of your job and lose the clock-watching aspects. Organisations like the Automobile Association have moved more and more of their employees out of offices and into their homes. Arm yourself with the experience of companies like this.

The computer programmer who switched to part-time work: *Anne is a graduate who joined a large national company with media and retailing businesses straight from university. She works as a computer programmer in Liverpool.*

When she had her first child Andrew she was back at work within six months. Part-time work was not an option at her firm at the time. Her husband was still a student and he did most of the daily childcare. Four years later when her second child Sarah was born, the climate of opinion had changed and she asked to switch to part-time work. Her boss agreed on the grounds that he would rather retain her skills than train and supervise someone else. But for Anne, it was also a question of money.

'All the registered childminders were very expensive. We couldn't afford it. I decided to work Mondays, Tuesdays and Wednesdays. My husband was still studying and he looked after Sarah those days. Sometimes we used a nursery as well. I looked after Sarah the other two days. It meant I had the contact of going out to work and keeping my hand in career-wise, but I still had four days at home so it always felt like I was at home more than I was at work which I was. It didn't feel like work took over my life.'

Persuading your boss

When you put the idea of flexible working to your employer it is useful to know that many organisations are experiencing a skills shortage. With near full employment, bosses are finding it difficult to recruit. Employers would rather keep part of you than have to recruit and train someone else.

The idea of switching to a three-day, thirty-hour week is easier to sell if you can find someone in your organisation who can take over on the other two days and deputise for you during holidays. You may even persuade your employers that this arrangement will actually work more smoothly than your present full-time arrangement. With new technologies such as e-mail, it may even be true. You can receive briefings on the next day's work at home and arrive fully prepared.

With some imagination, you may be able to earn three-quarters of your present pay and have four days at home every week. Many second- and third-time mothers work four ten-hour days, three at their companies' premises and one at home. That way they keep their full-time pay. To achieve this, however, they need to use professional childcare for at least three days. Once again, it is a matter of balancing income with expenditure.

More and more workplaces are introducing 'family-friendly' policies – flexible hours, job-sharing, homeworking, flexitime working and school hours or school-term working. You should explore them all and see which suits you best. It is almost never the right option to duck out and take welfare benefit. You lose your self-esteem. Far better to become a childminder and earn money from home while you look after your children (see page 139). At least then you are still a worker.

11: DISABLED CHILDREN

There are changes happening to help parents of disabled children in recognition of recent research under the auspices of the charity The Disability Alliance. This suggests that children can face developmental difficulties if their mobility needs are not met. The research indicates the social isolation which disabled children and their families can experience. The extra costs of disabled children are also highlighted in a Joseph Rowntree Foundation report *Paying to Care*, published in early 1998.

As a result, the government is about to allow parents of severely disabled children to take up to 13 weeks unpaid leave from work at any point until the child's 18th birthday. If you qualify, you will be able to take the leave a day at a time, rather than in week-long blocks like other employees.

The Government has announced a new Disability Income Guarantee which will ensure a weekly income of at least £199 for a family with one child who is severely disabled. This will benefit around 30,000 children in the UK.

There are also proposals to extend entitlement to the higher rate 'mobility component' of the Disability Living Allowance to three- and four-year-old severely disabled children with serious mobility problems. Currently it is available only to children aged over five. This help will be in addition to the new Disability Income Guarantee for those children with the highest care needs who are in the poorest families.

The extra help with mobility will also be available to those children aged three and four whose mobility is severely restricted as a result of childhood vaccines. This help will be neither means-tested nor taxable. It will provide an extra £35.85 a week, at April 1998 rates, to families with severely disabled three- and four-year-old children. It may also provide access to the Motability scheme.

You can ask for specific advice about your own entitlements at your local social security office.

The promise of part-time work that was not kept: *Jill worked as a PC analyst in Exeter for five years. She gave birth to William, a Down's syndrome baby, and returned to work part time, an arrangement she had agreed verbally early in her pregnancy. 'I'm sure we can sort something out,' said her boss, cheerfully. She needed as much time as possible to attend her son's appointments with the cardiologist, paediatrician, physiotherapist and psychologist. The sessions were between 10am and 3pm.*

But when her child was born, her employers wanted her back full time. They reluctantly agreed to let her work a three-day week, but only for three months. Before William's first birthday, she began to be pressured into returning to work full-time.

'Their justification is always "business need",' she wrote in a newsletter published by the charity Parents at Work. 'I put together a list of what I believed to be working solutions and finally got agreement that a job-share could be trialed, subject to finding a suitable candidate. Two months on, no suitable candidate has been located.'

Forced to return to full-time working, Jill took a day of annual leave a week to attend William's therapy sessions. Her employer finally offered her a four-and-a-half-day week, which Jill still found unacceptable. In desperation, she began to look for another job.

'William is already 25 per cent behind in his development,' she wrote. 'I am trying to juggle everything. I feel guilty for not giving him the time he needs. All I want is for my son to have the opportunity to achieve and for me to have the time to encourage him.'

Jill might have done better if she had got her employer's agreement in writing. Her boss would have then found it very embarrassing to go back on his word.

12: ADOPTED CHILDREN

Adoptive mothers are at a huge disadvantage compared with biological mothers. There is no equivalent of paid maternity leave, unless your employer is generous enough to offer it. Your only entitlement is 13 weeks' unpaid parental leave and standard Child Benefit. Some placing authorities give means-tested allowances, mostly to parents who adopt sibling groups.

This inequality of treatment is a major difficulty. Most adopted children have been in local authority care. They need considerable time to settle down with their new families. Parents also need time to form a bond with the child they have adopted. Meanwhile, parents are under pressure to return to work for financial reasons.

There is a major shortage of suitable adopters because of the economic penalties involved. The numbers have dropped from 2,300 to 2,000 a year. The number of adoptions has fallen from 21,000 in 1975 to below 6,000.

The British Agencies for Adoption and Fostering is campaigning for parity of treatment. A spokeswoman said: 'The government have offered the minimum. Some adopters have to take off three months unpaid leave. They may have taken more than one new child into their family. To lose a salary for three months makes things very difficult. For single people it is almost impossible. For some children who have lived with single parents, a single parent adopter would be ideal. Some children are nervous about living in a family where there is a man.'

Some employers such as BT UK offer paid leave for adoption, but there is no legal obligation to do so. In many parts of the country, individual schools within the same local education authority decide their own policies. A teacher in one school may be allowed paid leave, her or his equivalent in the next is not. With unsympathetic employers, the financial pressures on adoptive couples are enormous. One partner usually has to take unpaid parental leave to settle the adopted children into the family.

'It's not like maternity leave where you can plan ahead,' said Vicky Renwick of Adoption UK, the charity for adoptive parents. 'It can take years for a legal adoption to come through, and you do not know until the last minute if you are successful. Often there are two or three couples competing for the same child or children. When the Adoption Panel meets, any of them could be chosen. It is horrendously difficult for a working person to deal with that.

'When I adopted two children, I did not know if I would be successful until the day it happened. My boss had brought in somebody to replace me at great expense. But I could easily have had to tell him that I had not been successful and that I would have to carry on working. My colleagues organised a surprise party for me on the day I was to get the news. It went ahead at lunchtime, they had bought me presents, but I still had not been told if the match had gone ahead. Luckily it did and I left the next day.'

Making up for neglect: *Laura adopted Jenny and Sharon four years ago when she was working full time for the personnel department of Northampton Council. Jenny was four and her sister was eight. The girls had been in foster care for three years and had been badly neglected as babies. Sharon's teeth were badly decayed, she had almost no social skills, no friends and was seriously behind with her schoolwork. Her sister could not speak at all and needed therapy.*

'From the start, I knew I would have to take a lot of time off work,' said Laura. 'The four-year-old had to have speech therapy and physiotherapy. My eight-year-old had a lot of dental appointments because her teeth had been allowed to get so bad with her birth family. Now she's twelve and she's still three or four years behind.

'She had no social skills, she had never been to a friend's house for tea. For the first eight years of her life she missed out on such a lot. Now she's gone to secondary school, I'm finding it very difficult to cope. She's a nightmare at the moment. I'm forever being called into the school. She's hitting adolescence which is a major problem, but there are also a lot of problems about her adoption. The school doesn't always understand her behaviour.'

Laura took almost five months off work to settle her two daughters into the family. Luckily, her boss at Northampton Council was sympathetic and gave her the equivalent of ordinary maternity pay – 90 per cent of her average earnings for six weeks followed by the flat rate maternity pay for another twelve weeks. She was allowed to work school hours when she returned. She also gets an adoption allowance, thanks to a clever social worker and a generous placing authority. It is means-tested. She now works full time for a new employer who allows her to work two days from home.

'I am very lucky to have such an understanding employer,' she says. 'The children need me to be there. They've never had a mum or dad go to watch them in a school play. You make a concentrated effort to be there and that can be a problem, a lot of employers don't like that. My friends who have birth children accept that mum's working and she can't go. Mine would accept it but deep down it would destroy them because it would be another rejection. They've had so much rejection that we have to make sure we are there for them for everything they need. That can be hard juggling things around.

'Before Christmas I thought I had to give up work because I couldn't cope with everything, all this extra pressure on me to deal with my eldest daughter. I'm having behavioural problems at home stemming from school. I've got another review meeting next week with the school which means I've got to go there. It is very difficult when you work full time. I've got a cleaner now comes in once a week. You have to say hang on a minute I can't do it all, I'm not superwoman and something has to give. For me it's been the housework and the ironing.'

Unfairly treated: Tessa works as an incapacity benefits officer in Norfolk. As a civil servant she says she would have been entitled to 16 weeks maternity leave on full pay if she had become pregnant. As an adoptive parent, however, her paid leave was only 20 days.

'It's wrong that parents who adopt aren't given the same as birth mothers,' she said. 'I've worked for the department for 15 years and I feel discriminated against.'

Tessa and her husband Richard, who works as an alarm engineer, adopted Max, a 16-month-old boy. Two years later they adopted Nicole who was then six months old. They had waited a long time.

'For a year before I did not take any holiday. I accrued five or six weeks holiday, so I knew I'd got a couple of months with money. With the 20 days of adoptive leave pay, I knew I would have nine weeks of income. My husband wasn't particularly well-paid. I took another two-and-a-half months of unpaid leave. In all it came to five months, though I would have liked a year because he was a very difficult child.'

In the end, Tessa went back to work for two days a week and her husband's parents looked after Max. Her husband offered to give up his job to take over the childcare. This would have allowed her to go back full time.

But Tessa wanted to be a mother. She suggested that Richard work part time, but he felt he could not approach his employer with such a request.

'He's an electrician working as an alarm engineer. It's not the sort of occupation where you'd go in and say you'd like to go part time and share the childcare. Certain professions still have the building site type attitude of masculinity. He would have liked to have done it, but he felt he couldn't.

'I wanted the best of both worlds. I wanted to be a mum and a worker. Working two days a week was lovely, it gave me other interests rather than being at home all the time with a very demanding and quite difficult child. I also had a feeling of self worth. I enjoy my job. I enjoy the responsibility of it. 'My youngest child is two-and-a-half now. I'll go back four days a week when they're both at school. I think I'm a better mum because I do go to work; I think I have much more patience and time with the children when I'm at home.'

Tessa is still campaigning for parity of treatment over maternity leave. She has persuaded the civil servants' union to make it part of their policy.

13: SELF-EMPLOYED

There is no such thing as paid maternity leave for a self-employed mother. You merely lose the earnings you would have earned. Not surprisingly, self-employed mothers often take very little maternity leave, preferring the certainty of an income even if it means paying out for childcare when the baby is only a few weeks old.

You are entitled to Income Support if your income from all sources is below the minimum set by Parliament. If you are single, pregnant and unable to work, this is quite likely. You can claim from eleven weeks before the birth by visiting, phoning or writing to your local Benefits Agency office. Claims are normally accepted from the date the office receives your completed application form.

The amounts you can claim are not great, however; between £30.95 and £51.40 depending on your age. However, once your child is born you can claim for a dependent child as well – an extra £24.90. All parents, regardless of income, are entitled to Child Benefit, currently £15.50 a week for the first child.

The main problem for most self-employed mothers is managing to work while your baby is young. Some mothers find novel solutions.

The baby who went to school: *Chloe had set up a new small private school in London with a former colleague when she realised that she was pregnant. The school opened in late April 1997 and her baby was born in February 1998. She worked until Christmas and was back at work again after Easter – with her baby, Georgia, aged three months.*

Because she was a partner in her own business, she could take a more flexible approach to child care. A backup teacher joined her in the classroom while Georgia slept on a playmat in the corner. When she needed feeding, Chloe took her into a private room while the assistant kept an eye on her class.

'I found it a struggle at first to concentrate on what I was doing,' said Chloe. 'She would wake up and cry from time to time and I would have to take her out. In the end, however, you just have to get on with your job. If you are controlling a group of ten to twelve children, you have to do it.

'I tried having someone else looking after Georgia for a time, but it did not work. When she cried I had to see what was going on and deal with it. After a term, Georgia was six months old and I found it quite a chore ferrying all her baby things back and forward every day. I decided to find someone to look after her at home.

'Again I was lucky. My business partner's wife, Bea, had a four-year-old boy, Buster. She took Georgia in a pushchair every morning to Buster's school, then looked after Georgia the rest of the day.'

Chloe does the administrative work for her school at home, where Georgia can make as much noise as she likes. She thinks the pupils have gained by having a baby at school. Over two years, they have watched Georgia's development with interest.

'The girls and the older boys have shown most interest,' she said. 'One of the mothers asked me to show her eleven-year-old son how to change Georgia's nappy. I think she thought it would be a good lesson in responsibility. Two of the girls were so keen on looking after Georgia that I could offer it to them as a prize for good behaviour.

Some of the younger boys did not like all aspects of having a baby at school. They complained about having to be unnaturally quiet. Georgia on the other hand seemed to thrive.

'She seemed to enjoy the stimulation of all the pupils around her, the sights and sounds were good for her. The only disadvantage was that she caught a lot of colds because she did not have much immunity. She had illnesses all through the summer. But it seems to have toughened her up. From the age of one she has been extremely healthy.'

Chloe's business partner Garth has been very supportive. Chloe had told him that she was wanting to start a family before they began their new school.

'We had been trying for a baby for a year and a half,' she said. 'It was just my luck that I conceived a week after the school opened. I had to take a step back from teaching and the long working hours for at least a term. But I still spent a lot of time discussing details of how the school was running and interviewing new pupils who wanted to join. I could also do a lot of administration from home.'

'If I have a second child, I shall employ a full-time nanny. I don't think Georgia lost out when I returned to work full time. She was six months old and she had Bea to look after her one-to-one. I think that's the important thing, that you trust the carer and that the baby can have full-time attention.'

In retrospect, Chloe does not think she should have tried to teach and look after her child at the same time. The two activities are not compatible. She was very lucky that her business partner's wife could help her out. Her real problem was that before the birth she was too busy concentrating on setting up her business to do proper research into childcare. Under such circumstances, it would have been a risk to choose a nursery or childminder. If her plans had changed, she would have had to start looking all over again.

A nanny is a much better solution for many self-employed mothers because home is a more constant factor. For many women, working from home with a professional childcarer in the background is the ideal solution.

The businesswoman who 'commuted' upstairs: *Susan was running two businesses from her home in West London when her second daughter Sarah was born. She separated her job from her role as mother. She employed a live-out nanny who arrived at eight every morning – an hour ahead of her secretary.*

Susan's main job was as a personnel officer for the UK division of a large multinational business machine corporation. The company had decided to sell off some of its central London offices and put key management personnel on contract, working from home. At the same time, it helped them set up their own businesses – with an undertaking that the new business should represent 50 per cent of income within five years. Susan chose car leasing.

When she was setting up the business, she could manage most of the work from the spare bedroom of her home, which was turned into an office with high-speed computer links.

'I made a conscious choice not to rent an office because I knew I wanted another child,' she said. 'I wanted to simplify my life as much as I could. It meant that when Sarah was born, I could carry on working within a week. My secretary would arrive as normal and answer all the calls. I could give her guidance and keep most of the business ticking over by just being there. I started going to business meetings after about a month.

'Sarah is now two and her sister Naomi is four. Their nanny arrives first and I hand them over to her. I separate my working life from my home life at 9am,' she said. 'I say goodbye to the children when my secretary arrives. Then I go upstairs to work until lunchtime. The children are not allowed upstairs except in emergencies. But they have the security of knowing that mum is nearby.'

Susan organised her way out of trouble. She also separated her role as mother from her role as worker. Few people can achieve this in their own home, especially if they can hear their children playing in the background. Susan was disciplined. She shut the door and pretended she was miles away.

It is interesting to note that most of Susan's colleagues failed to work from home and start up a business. Many of them found offices near to home and travelled to them every day so that they could separate work and home life.

Nannies are not for everyone, either. Some self-employed mothers find it impossible to hand their children over to a mother-subsititute whether it is a nanny or a childminder. In the case of Rachel, it forced her to work from home to look after her own child.

The jealous mother: *Rachel and her husband ran a successful franchise business selling and servicing upmarket televisions and hi-fi in South London. When her baby Natasha was born, she found a live-out nanny. She returned to work, travelling each day to the showroom where she dealt with the administrative and marketing side of the family business.*

But after six months, she found it more and more difficult to leave her child with the nanny. 'I was jealous,' she said. 'It seemed to me that I was missing out. I wanted to be with my daughter all the time. In the end I told the nanny that I would no longer need her because I had reorganised my working day so that I could do more work from home.' Rachel installed a computer link between her home and the office and did the administration for the business while keeping an eye on Natasha.

'It is very difficult sometimes because you can be in the middle of a phone call when the baby starts crying. But it's not a major problem because it's our own business. No-one is going to criticise me for being unprofessional.

'I have a mother's help who comes in every day to clean and look after Natasha for a few hours when I have to go and see clients. It's a much better balance than I had before.'

A few mothers give up self-employment when they have children for similar reasons. Like Rachel, they cannot stand the idea of a nanny monopolising their child's affections. Gilly, a freelance designer I know, had worked successfully from home for five years when her daughter, Phoebe, was born. But she could not bear to be in the house at the same time as her nanny. She found herself distracted by the sounds of

Phoebe playing. She only managed to work when they went for a walk or the baby was asleep. Gilly gave up work to care for her baby. She was fortunate enough to be married to a successful businessman. She had another child and plans to return to work when they are both at school.

Becoming self-employed for the family's sake

A few mothers decide to become self-employed when they have children because it allows them to stay at home. Becoming a childminder is the classic way to achieve this (see page 139). Other attempts to become self-employed only make sense if you can guarantee your income. Most mothers would not risk such a move unless their partner earned enough for them to get by if things went wrong.

However, if you are good at your job and it can be done on a freelance basis, there is nothing to stop you approaching your boss and asking if there is a reasonable chance of working for him or her on a self-employed basis. For an employer it can make more sense than adjusting your job to part-time employment. It is less formal. It may be more flexible if you agree to work harder during peak times. But being freelance means you should also find at least one more employer. It is dangerous to have all your eggs in one basket. You must never be dependent on one source of income. It may put your freelance status in jeopardy.

Self-employed for the children's sake: Penny Hughes was president of the UK division of Coca Cola for two years. She earned a quarter of a million pounds a year. She was destined to become one of the company's highest flyers when, at the age of 34, she became self-employed to have a family.

Before her first child Alex was born, she took on a non-executive directorship with the Body Shop. In the following four years, she took on another three non-executive directorships including Vodaphone, the mobile telephone company. She employs a nanny so that she can work from home. But she takes her two sons aged three and four to the doctor and playschool herself.

'I do have quite a lot of business responsibilities. I get time to be at my desk most days at home. Some people who ring up get my three-year-old, but it amuses rather than offends. It's acceptable. Sometimes I say, I'm sorry I'm with the children, I'll have to ring you back. It's probably been easier for me to retain some corporate network and corporate responsibilities being a

155

woman because I stand out from the crowd. It was an easier decision for me to make than for men.'

She will continue her present working arrangements until her two sons become old enough for primary school. It means that she will be ideally placed to run a business again.

Good childcare was the key to Penny Hughes's choice of self-employment. Without a nanny she could rely on, she could not have contemplated business trips to the USA for several days at a time, for example. They may have been few and far between, but she needed to know that her child was taken care of as well as if she had been at home to see to them herself.

Nurseries for babies

Nurseries are becoming a more common choice for self-employed new mothers. In the last few years, many private nurseries have opened 'baby rooms' for children as young as two months. Some self-employed mothers prefer them because they offer a more clear-cut division between work and childcare.

The nursery and the new business: *Jayne was pregnant when she and her husband were looking for a site for their new business – a full-service sign-making company supplying everything from stickers on vans to shop fascias. They found the perfect spot in Armley in West Leeds. Their home was four miles away in the north-west suburbs of the city.*

Jayne began looking for childcare which was convenient for work and home. But she chose what at first glance looks like the most difficult option.

She ruled out a nanny because one of her best friends had recently employed a trained nanny who had bullied her child badly. She ruled out childminders after visiting several and finding the mix of children not to her liking. 'I thought the range of ages was too great.,' she said. 'Some had new-born babies up to pre-school. I didn't like that particular mix.'

She then started researching nurseries. After seeing more than a dozen, she picked the least convenient – a nursery in Rawdon six miles from her new business. It meant travelling two miles in the wrong direction from home every morning to drop off her baby daughter Holly, who was born six months after the new business opened. In the morning rush hour the journey took her almost an hour.

'It sounds crazy, but if you've got any doubts about your childcare I don't think you can concentrate on your work. I went to one nursery about four times. It was much more convenient than the one we chose, it was on the way from home to work, but there was something not right for us. There was a certain teaching methodology, they made the kids go outside when it was cold and when I took Gary he agreed.'

'We thought it was better for me to travel all the way to Rawdon even though we were starting a new business because the nursery was so nice. They cuddle your kids and they kiss them when they've had an accident. They have a baby room, a toddler room, a three-year-olds room and a pre-school room. I really like that idea. The people who look after your baby are the same people each time. They have to have a different care ratio for babies. One employee for two babies.

'Nurseries have taken on a whole new dimension now, they've taken over from nannies and childminders in some ways. They're just so set up for the different ages. They have different toys, they even have different objectives that they try to achieve with the babies every day. You get a slip, a report at the end of every day telling you what your child's been doing, what she's eaten what she hasn't. You get a really detailed insight of what's been going on. I drop her off at 8.30 and pick her up at 1.30 in the afternoon. But she wants to go all day now because she loves it and she's coming up to three. It wasn't easy but once you have the peace of mind that you like the place your child goes to, you can get on with your job.'

Jayne looks after the marketing side of the business while her husband Gary runs the operational side. They employed a graphic designer and over the past two years they have taken on two more employees.

'It is a juggle and the hardest thing is to pack your bags up at a quarter past one and go home and think about different priorities. I do a lot of work on a night. I go back to work a couple of afternoons a week because my mother-in-law now takes Holly out in the park and all that sort of thing. You have to be unbelievably organised.'

Holly is now almost three and Jayne is pregnant again. The baby is due around the time she is speaking at a conference for small businesses.

'If by any chance I do have a baby early, my husband will be able to step into my shoes, and we do have to double up a little like that. We do anyway because I'm not here in the afternoons. We've divided our roles now. Saturdays and Sundays are just for the family. You've got to put time aside. We've learned that over a long period of time.'

14: COUNTRY DWELLERS

Rural areas are among the harshest environments in which working mothers can raise children. There are simply not enough people around to form the support system you need. Nannies and au pairs do not want to live in the country because they feel isolated. Nurseries are miles away in the nearest towns. Childminders are also comparatively rare. By and large, you have to take what you can find or set up a scheme of your own.

Mother's helps

If you can work from home, you may be able to find yourself a mother's help from your own village or area. Mother's helps are not nannies. They are not even trained in childcare. They are women who like looking after children but who are also prepared to do the household chores such as cleaning and ironing. The wages you need to pay are a little more than those a cleaner would earn in your area. Choose someone you know well and trust. The idea is that you work from home while the mother's help keeps an eye on the children and does some housework at the same time. In your spare time, you look after the children, while the mother's help does the chores you could not do because of your childcare responsibilities.

The difficulties come if you need to work away from home. You cannot leave your child in the sole charge of a mother's help, unless you have very good reason to think that person is capable of doing the job. A nurse who had young children of her own and had taken a career break might be the ideal person to help you out, for example. However, you are effectively looking for a nanny. The problem is that nannies do not often want to live in the country. They tend to be young and in need of the company of people their own age. It is much more difficult to find such company unless you are in a large village or a small town.

I have known one trained nanny turn down the offer of a job in the country even though it came with a new car and a salary equal to that of a junior manager. She was 20 and she liked her circle of friends in the big city. The employer was in the music business and offered her an apartment of her own in a large country mansion, but she decided that she would not have a full social life. She opted to stay put in the city on a much smaller income.

Au pairs

Some families settle for au pairs. This is dangerous. An au pair is not a nanny. She is little more than a schoolgirl who has come to Britain to learn English. She is not capable of being left in sole charge of pre-school children. She also needs your company. Someone who goes out to work every day is not the kind of employer she needs. The entire purpose of being an au pair is to have daily conversations in the language of the country she chooses, preferably backed up by language courses at a nearby college.

The au pair's country nightmare: John and Pam worked in television in London. They lived, however, in a small village in East Anglia. Every day during the working week, they would rise at 5.30 and drive to the station at Kettering to take the train to King's Cross. The children were still asleep as they left. It was not until 7pm that they returned.

They employed a succession of au pairs to look after their two daughters aged seven and nine. Most were from Eastern Europe. Most lasted no more than two or three months. They stayed slightly longer if they arrived in the warm summer months. Each au pair was overwhelmed by the luxury of their accommodation at first. They had a room of their own with its own bathroom. But being in sole charge of school-age children soon became too much of a strain.

The children resented being ordered around by teenage girls with limited English. The au pairs resented being left in sole charge. After taking the girls to school every day in the car, they would be left alone in the house to do the washing, ironing and cleaning. The sense of isolation was overwhelming. Attempts at making contacts with other people in the village almost all ended in failure. The village had no shops, nowhere to meet any other teenagers. Most contacted their agencies and asked for another placement – in a large town or a city where they could meet young people of their own age.

This experience is repeated all over Britain. Some au pair agencies are reluctant to send girls to families in rural areas unless there are exceptional circumstances which make it possible for them to settle in and have a social life and a real opportunity to learn English. The cost of finding them another placement is considerable. The emotional cost of making them miserable is even greater.

Childminders

The most popular form of childcare in rural areas is the childminder. Your council's social services department will have a list of the ones nearest to you. Unlike city dwellers, you will have to make a compromise between suitability and distance. The most suitable childminder may be miles away. You will almost certainly need to buy a car if you are to deliver your child on your way to work. If you cannot drive, move to a village where a childminder is registered.

The illegal childminder: Even those who work full-time in childcare can sometimes have problems. Lynn worked as a registration officer for childminders, but could not find one for her own child.

'When I had my first daughter twelve years ago, all the registered minders in the area where I lived were totally full,' she said. 'Even going to the areas around, there was nowhere available. I used someone who at that point was an illegal minder. She was a qualified teacher who had no idea she had to register. I heard by word of mouth that she was looking after children. I asked the questions and ended up persuading her to register for me. She ended up registered within three months.

'It was so uncomfortable because I was supposed to be enforcing these regulations and I couldn't find anybody. Had she refused me I don't know what I would have done because she was the perfect person for my daughter. But what choice would I have had?'

Childminders can take up to six children under the age of eight. They can, in theory, take as many children as they like above that age, though most local authorities advise a limit of ten children. Until 2000, they were inspected each year by the local social services department, a responsibility now handed to the schools' inspectorate, OFSTED. Their premises must be safe and most local authorities insist on a minimum course of training (see page 23).

Plans are afoot to let grandparents register as childminders. If you know of a local family where grandparents are looking after their own grandchildren, it might be possible to persuade them to train and register as childminders so that they can look after your children, too. The normal rate is around £2 to £2.50 an hour per child.

Neighbours as childcarers

If you are not prepared to move house to be near a nursery or a childminder, the only real alternative is to look for help among your neighbours. This depends entirely on your social skills. If you are good at making friends, you may be able to establish a network of neighbours who will look after your children while you are at work or whose sons or daughters can collect your children from school and baby-sit for a few hours each day. Other mothers with children of a similar age to your own are often the best bet for full-time care during the day. They may not have considered becoming unofficial childminders, but would welcome the extra income it might bring.

With the government drive to professionalise childcare as much as possible, it might be a good idea to offer to pay a neighbour with pre-school children to register as an official childminder so that she can look after your children while you are at work. That way, you can be sure that her home has been checked for hazards by the authorities – particularly if your children are toddlers. Unguarded ponds and greenhouses can lead to fatal accidents. The pre-registration training is not rigorous, often no more than two hours a week for a month.

As a registered childminder, your neighbour isn't obliged to take in anyone else's children unless she wants to do so. She has no need to advertise or do anything more than stick to her arrangement with you. The advantage to her is that it puts your relationship on a more businesslike footing. She can set an hourly rate. She will not feel exploited if you are late from work. Of course, she will have to pay tax on her earnings – but not unless they are over a certain threshold.

If she is not prepared to put up with such officialdom, there is nothing to stop you finding out the guidelines about safety in childminders' premises for yourself and making your own house a safe house. Then you can invite the other mother to look after both families there. Alternatively, you can offer to pay for the same improvements to be made to her premises. That way you can both have peace of mind.

15: THE WORKER RETURNS

Your workplace is never the same when you return. Your absence during maternity leave is bound to make your colleagues form new ways of working which do not depend on you. When you return, they may not want things to go back to the way they were.

You are different, too. The experience of childbirth is so life-changing that you can never see the world in the same way again. You can no longer think of yourself as just an individual who does a job. You are now someone with responsibility for another human existence, someone with a network of new friends and helpers who know you in your other role – as a mother.

The trick about returning to work is to make it seem as if you have never been away. If you stay in touch with your workmates throughout your maternity leave, there will be no shock when you finally return. Think of it in terms of holidays. When you were at work, everyone had to adjust constantly to the absence of their co-workers who were on holiday. If you had a query which only your absent colleague could answer, you would wait. Not to worry, you might say. Jane will be back in ten days, we can ask her then. However, what if Jane's holiday was four weeks long, and a few of the queries were rather important. You would not wait for her return. You would find out the answers some other way. You would begin to do without Jane. If Jane's holiday stretched to two months, you would learn to dispense with her altogether.

Maternity leave is no different. The reason for your absence is irrelevant. Your brilliance (or otherwise) as a worker is irrelevant. The only thing that matters is that you are not there as part of the team and that those who are left have to get on with things without you.

In theory, (finances permitting), you could take 40 weeks off for maternity leave, eleven weeks before the birth and another 29 after it. This means you could have a leaving party in October and not return until the following July. Three seasons would have passed. An entire new generation of recruits would have arrived who do not even know who you are. One of them could be doing your job. If things are going well, your return might not be entirely welcome.

Your employment rights entitle you to your old job back. But your old job may no longer exist. If your boss decides to 'restructure' the organisation, you could end up sidelined. Your employer must offer you equivalent work or redundancy. But what if the 'equivalent' job turns out to be just a fancy title and no substance? What if you hate your new role? Some unscrupulous employers will use this ruse to force you to resign.

Ten golden rules

For this reason, I have devised the ten golden rules for preparing your return to work. They are designed, among other things, to give you early warning signals about threats to your job and your relationships with your colleagues. If you spot the danger signs, you can then take action to limit the damage. However, if you are approaching the end of your maternity leave, you will have to move fast to put some of them into practice.

Rule 1: Agree a plan of return. You should have done this before you started maternity leave. If you did not, take your boss to lunch (without your baby) as soon as possible and discuss the timetable of your return to work. Be constructive. Think of ways you can help your colleagues out while you are away. Offer to do some work from home to ease your way back into work. Be positive and enthusiastic about your return. Look more like a worker than a mother (even though you may not feel like it). Come up with solutions about how you will fit in childcare with work.

Rule 2: Get it in writing. The next day, send your boss a letter summarising your verbal agreement and ask him to sign.

Rule 3: Stick to your agreed timetable. If things go wrong, give as much advance warning as you can.

Rule 4: It is a good idea for your sanity and your relationships to have some outings without your baby, long before you return to work. Arrange it with the nursery or childcarer you have chosen to look after your baby when you return to work. Do this well in advance of your return so that you can get used to the idea that your baby can be left safely. It may only be a couple of hours one lunchtime when you go to the local pizza restaurant, but it is good practice for leaving the baby and getting used to the idea that you can go away and return to find that all is well.

Rule 5: Keep in touch with your deputy and other colleagues during the early weeks of motherhood. If you can, help them out from home. Become your deputy's 'deputy'. Supply useful information. Be humble, helpful and cheerful. Do not undermine their decisions.

Rule 6: Visit your workplace within a month. This is important. It keeps you in everyone's minds' eye as a colleague who is coming back. If your workplace is 'family-unfriendly', do not bring your baby with you. Photographs are fine, but only produce them if you are asked. The aim is to show interest in your colleagues' progress and offer to help out from home. Do not stay too long or get in the way of their work.

Rule 7: Take your close work friends out to lunch or for a drink, preferably every two or three weeks during your maternity leave. The idea is to catch up on gossip. Be alert to any threat to your job.

Rule 8: If your substitute is stealing your job, arrange to meet your boss for a 'friendly' chat. Mention your written agreement.

Rule 9: Spend a day at work in the week before your return. Use your visit as a dry-run to test your childcare arrangements. Use it also to make sure your work clothes fit. Prepare yourself and your colleagues for the role you are about to resume and your new 'flexible' working hours. Be friendly and helpful, but keep a watchful eye for signs of hostility. Do not talk about your baby unless someone shows an interest. Colleagues without children often find the subject irritating. Some may also resent your new status as a mother and your new 'privileged' work pattern. Allow yourself time to talk to a temporary replacement or whoever is covering for you. You need to find out if there have been any changes to paperwork, procedures, personalities.

Rule 10: On the day of your real return, be there an hour early. If you are organised and ready to hit the ground running by the time your colleagues turn up, they can hardly fail to be impressed.

The Return

The longer you have been out of the workplace, the stranger your
return will seem and the more you are likely to miss your baby.

Mothers who have ignored golden rule number four often find the
trauma of separation huge. They feel lost without their babies. Their
babies feel lost without them. Their childcarers have to cope with tears
for days, if not weeks. The feelings of guilt caused by this lack of
preparation can be very destructive. It can make a mother feel that
what she is doing is against the child's best interests.

The suspicion arises that some mothers engineer unsatisfactory
childcare to give themselves an excuse for staying at home, or working
from home. Occasionally, this may be because they are too cowardly or
too embarrassed to ask their bosses or colleagues for more flexible
working arrangements.

*Too embarrassed to work less: Emily worked as marketing director for
a media company in London. She was at the top of her profession when her
son Archie was born. Her husband had a good income and she could have
afforded to work part time or take a career break. Instead, she continued
with her full-time job. She regarded giving up her status and responsibilities
as defeat.*

*She could have afforded a nanny or a childminder, too, but she chose
not to. By the time Archie was four, she and her husband had taken full
responsibility for accompanying him to and from nursery school, despite
the fact that the demands of her job often made this very difficult.*

*She admitted that she failed to discuss her problems frankly with her
colleagues. Her company had family-friendly policies and several of its
directors worked flexible hours to cope with childcare. She thought she could
cope. But she took days off when Archie was ill, and tried to work from
home. She even sent him to nursery school when he was ill.*

*Eventually, her company changed her job during restructuring. She
resigned and became a successful freelance, working from home.*

In the end, Emily got what she needed, though she tried to convince
herself for a long time that it was not what she wanted. It can be very
hard to give up a high-status job when you have set yourself up as a
role model. However, if she had found the courage to talk honestly
with her colleagues and her partner, she could have almost certainly

worked out a compromise that would have retained the best parts of her job with no loss of face, while allowing her to look after her son.

Tiredness

Physical exhaustion is a problem for most mothers who return to work full time. When one of my colleagues, Sally, went back to work after her first child was born, she could not believe how tired she was at the end of an eight- or nine-hour day. She was in her twenties and thought she was fit.

'No one had warned me,' she said. 'I would trudge up the hill going home from the station and wonder what on earth I was doing wrong. I had got through those early weeks when nights were totally disrupted and I was feeling even more tired. I used to go into the office loo in the afternoon and almost fall asleep because I was so tired. It was awful.'

For that very reason, you should not expect too much of yourself. If you are tense, your baby will be tense. It is not unusual for babies who sleep through the night to start waking more when their mothers are anxious. Some even refuse to go to sleep at all when their mothers try to settle them down at night. It is difficult to know what advice to give in such circumstances. If you let the baby cry, your sleep will be shallow and you will wake up feeling dreadful. If you stay to comfort your child, you will be exhausted. Either way, you lose.

It may be possible to stagger your return so that in the first weeks you do some of the work from home and some from the office. I did this and it worked well. It may allow you a gentler departure in the morning or time in the evening to play with your child. Trying to rush either end of the day is a recipe for tension and grief.

When the Big Day comes, you must prepare for a physical shock. After life in the warm cocoon of your family home, returning to work is bracing. You have spent weeks with your baby, carrying out the gentle routines of feeding, changing and bathing. Now you will have to snap out of it, look sharp, put on your work clothes and face the world. If you are a commuter, you may have to be breakfasted, dressed and out by 7.30 every morning, ready to take your baby to the childminder. You can no longer doze on after your partner has left as you did before. If you had a difficult night, tough! Think yourself awake! Become the worker you once were!

If I am sounding like a drill sergeant, it is because some mothers do lose sight of the discipline of the working day. What is worse, in offices where women predominate, a first baby can confer a kind of temporary celebrity status on you which can make you complacent. This is not good. Luckily, it does not usually last long. Your colleagues will soon tire of looking at your photographs of baby's first bath, baby's first clothes and baby's first wind. There is work to be done, after all.

Adjusting to changes at work

In most cases you will be going back into your old job with the same old friends and enemies. But your relationships will have changed with the passing of time. You may experience a sense of unreality. I have talked to mothers who describe their return after six to eight months as like living in slow-motion. Even sound seems distorted. It is as if they are living in a memory. I have no explanation for this, though I feel sure that it is something to do with our perception of time. Time during maternity leave has a different rhythm.

You must make sure that you know all the new faces who have been recruited since you went away. Introduce yourself to them. They also need to get to know you. Some people may have left. There could have been restructuring. Your boss might have been promoted into another part of the company. Your department might have moved to another part of the building or your desk moved to fit more people in.

It is quite possible that your desk may no longer be yours. It may have been squatted during your absence. The chances are that your stapler, Sellotape dispenser and all the other essentials will have been permanently 'borrowed'. Your plant may have died or be thriving on someone else's desk. You cannot be too precious. Remember you left them in the lurch. They had to do your job – usually for no extra pay – and now you are back as if nothing has happened.

If you have kept in touch with your boss and colleagues you should know of any significant changes. If you have had material sent home you should not come in to find a towering pile of paper in your in tray, or the even sadder prospect of a few old, yellowing scraps of paper from your last day in the office.

For many mothers who have spent months in sweatshirts and leggings, the biggest shock is getting back into suits or other smart office wear. Do not assume that they will fit. The winter suit with the wider waistband that you had when you were four months pregnant may be out of place in May. It is worth having a session with your wardrobe to see what fits, what is still fashionable and what you feel good in.

A shopping trip may be the answer to make you feel good about yourself as a worker. If you have not got back to your old shape, do not buy clothes in the hope that the weight/inches will drop off in the next few weeks. Do not give up, either. Once you are away from the biscuit tin and lots of milky drinks you should find things begin to tighten up. You can always have the incentive of another shopping trip to look forward to. If money is tight, you may have to move a button, borrow an outfit or wear a long jacket to effect a disguise.

Coping with childcare

What you can manage at work will depend on the support system you have in place. You do not have to do it all, especially if you have a partner. You can take turns to do the housework, the shopping, the laundry or the babycare. Better still, if you are working full time and you can afford it, hire a cleaner and ask her or him to do the ironing.

It is a mistake to keep checking up on your baby all day. It is a terrible distraction. It will drive your colleagues nuts. It will only make you more anxious, too. What is your childcarer supposed to say when you ring up and say: 'How's my baby?'. If she has any sense she will simply say 'Fine'. If your baby has been crying all morning, and she has tried and failed to get the wailing to stop, it would be unprofessional of her to worry you with the news. A childcarer's duty is to solve problems not to create new ones. One of my colleagues called her nanny ten times for progress reports during her first day back. All she succeeded in doing was making herself more anxious and her nanny more insecure.

Some nurseries in the United States are now installing cameras to reassure mothers. It is only a matter of time before they arrive in Britain (see page 48). Recent developments in internet technology mean that web cameras may soon be cheap enough to install in the work premises of nurseries, childminders, or even in your own home so that you can look in on a nanny. I think they are a bad idea for two reasons. The first is that they are unlikely to give you enough information to be useful. You can easily misinterpret what is happening on the screen. You can become worried for no reason. If you keep telephoning your childcarer for reassurance, you damage the relationship with her.

The second reason is that watching the pictures from web cameras all day may get you fired, particularly if you use your employer's equipment to do it. You may be in breach of your contract about the misuse of computers for non-work purposes. In extreme cases you could even be fired for failing to do your job if you spend too much time checking up on your child.

Childhood illnesses worry a lot of new mothers, especially when they are at work. They fear that their childcarer will not spot the symptoms of a potentially serious condition and that by the time they arrive home, things will have gone from bad to worse.

When I was expecting my first baby I took great comfort from a magazine publisher who told me that in ten years as a working mother she had been called home for a medical emergency only once. My own experience has been much the same. I have also been called once for a sick child in eleven years. My youngest boy had been quiet on the way to school and by lunchtime he had a temperature and did not want to eat. My nanny was out shopping so the school called me. It was worth it to see the look on his face when I arrived to take him home and to wait until the nanny returned.

The increased use of mobile phones means that most childcarers can now be contacted no matter where they are with your children. But that does not mean I regret going to pick my child up and cherish him when he was feeling poorly.

The more you ring to check on your child's health, the more likely that the carer will over-react. She will begin to worry about the smallest blemish or runny nose. If your child is with a capable carer she will be just as vigilant as you, but probably calmer.

NHS Direct

There is now another reason for working mothers to worry less – the advent of the new nurse-led, 24-hour telephone advice and information service called NHS Direct. This service, which offers round-the-clock access to information and advice about health, illness and health services, will cover the whole of England by the end of 2000. There is one number for the entire country – 0845 46 47. It is charged at local rates.

The telephone lines are answered locally by experienced nurses who are specially trained to give advice over the phone. They ask you or your childcarer a series of questions which, with the aid of a powerful computer program, helps them decide how serious your child's problem is. They then advise you if you need to seek further medical help and direct you to the appropriate service, for example your GP or the local hospital's accident and emergency department.

In the areas where it has been in operation for the past year, the majority of calls have been from mothers with young children. Many have been worried that their children have meningitis. The nurses have asked the mothers to carry out straightforward tests, and have been mostly able to reassure the mothers that their worries are unfounded. In the rare cases where the symptoms of meningitis are present, the emergency services have been called and the child has been rushed to hospital.

If you are sidelined

It is comforting to think that only high-flyers risk being sidelined by maternity leave, but even low-paid jobs are at risk. I have seen this from both sides, as an employee-observer and as a boss.

It is quite possible that while you are away, your boss may decide to change the way your department is run, to promote some people, move others sideways and make some redundant. This is a perfectly legitimate business practice.

Your old job may no longer exist after such restructuring. If your job disappears you are only entitled to 'alternative employment' rather than your old job. This alternative work must be suitable and appropriate for you to do in the circumstances. It must also have terms and conditions which are 'not substantially less favourable' to you than under your previous contract.

In other words, you should be offered another job which fits your skills. There is a lot of interpretation to be done, however, to decide what is 'suitable and appropriate' to you and what constitutes 'substantially less favourable' terms and conditions. If you are a senior manager, a middle-ranking manager's post may fit your skills, but your employer is breaking the law if your pay or perks are cut according to your new, more lowly rank.

This is a very difficult situation for anyone to bear, particularly if someone else seems to be doing your old job under a new title. There may be little you can do, however, except grin and bear it. The time for action was when the changes were being discussed. If you had kept more closely in touch with your colleagues, you might have been tipped off and you could have appeared in person to fight your corner. If it happens to you, you should consult your union, trade association or a lawyer. But best of all you should prevent it.

What may be even worse is when someone takes your job from under your nose. You have to think yourself into your employer's mind. You have gone on maternity leave and in her or his opinion your temporary replacement is better at your job than you were. What does the employer do? Ignore the improvements made by your temporary successor and offer you your old job back?

Well, yes, as a matter of law. Under the Employment Relations Act 1999 you are entitled to 'the same job and the same terms and conditions' as if you had not been absent. It does not matter that your boss thinks your replacement was better at it, it is your job and you are entitled to return to it. However, your sense of security may be short-lived. There is nothing to stop your boss moving you to a new department shortly after your return.

Sidelined: *Georgia was the personal assistant to a director of a large national corporation with headquarters in South London. She told her boss in writing that she was pregnant and that she intended to return to work six months after the baby was born. She started her maternity leave in July, four weeks before the birth of her second baby, Sam.*

A temporary secretary was brought in to do her job – Lynn. She was looking for a full-time job and wanted to become a management trainee, but had made it clear that she would accept secretarial work as a temporary measure. She had worked for the firm three times during her university holidays, twice as a temporary replacement for Georgia. She was very good at her job, so good that the director wanted her instead of Georgia. She put the idea to Lynn and Lynn agreed.

This was entirely legal. Georgia was entitled to her old job back after her maternity leave. However, she was not entitled to keep it if her company decided to transfer her to an equivalent post elsewhere in the business.

Georgia was interviewed shortly after her return. Her boss told her that the company had decided to move her to another department. The terms and conditions of her employment would be unaltered. Georgia was devastated. 'I felt they should have given me some warning. I felt really humiliated. I had done the job for four years and I was being told I was no longer wanted. I thought my boss was deceitful.'

'She should have spoken to me while I was on maternity leave and called me in for a chat or something. She waited till I got back and said they were reorganising the department. It just wasn't true. It was really only my job that was being reorganised. She said she'd really appreciated my work, but I felt very let down. I was transferred to a totally different department within a week. I felt really depressed. It took all the joy out of having my baby.'

Georgia worked in her new department for the next seven months and then left after finding a part-time job nearer home.

Georgia's only real mistake was her failure to keep in touch with office gossip during her maternity leave. If she had, she would not have been so shocked to find herself replaced. She had complied with all the rules about giving her boss warning of when she planned to return. She had kept her promises. It is likely that what happened was only brought forward by her maternity leave. Her boss had already spotted the potential of her replacement when she worked as a temporary secretary during holiday periods.

16: CHANGING JOBS

Changing jobs may, in some circumstances, help you cope with childcare far better than trying to make your existing job fit your new responsibilities. This is particularly true if you have a high-flyer's job in a business where male long-hours culture prevails. Several recent cases have shown that employers in major financial and legal institutions expect well-paid women to sacrifice their families for their jobs, just as their male colleagues have done for years.

If you fail to negotiate more flexible working hours or to persuade your employer that you could do part of your job instead of the whole, there may be little choice left than to find a new job which is more suited to motherhood. There are two approaches. The first is the most radical – to switch careers.

From lawyer to healer: *Lyndsey Booth was a distinguished lawyer like her famous sister, Cherie, the wife of the British prime minister. She had worked for 15 years as a top property lawyer, earning a six-figure salary. But when she was eight months' pregnant she decided to give it all up and retrain as a homeopath.*

'They were not prepared for any proper maternity leave, so I used to feed the baby through the night and struggle to keep awake during the day,' she told her local newspaper, the Highbury and Islington Express. 'I regret so many years spent in such a heavily driven environment with such a lack of concern for people's lives.'

The crunch came when she had spent an entire evening negotiating a property deal. It was midnight and she had finally won through. Her male boss, ignoring her pregnancy, insisted that they went out to celebrate. She refused. 'Even the client was shocked by his attitude and put me into the taxi home himself,' she said.

She said she decided to change jobs to something less profit-driven. She wanted something that would benefit both herself and her family.

'A lawyer's life isn't in any way conducive to family life,' she said. 'When I was pregnant and a scan appointment clashed with a business meeting, it certainly wasn't the client who was cancelled. Around the office,

people would comment that I wasn't committed enough. It was impossible. I was stressed and rushed everything.'

She could have afforded a full-time nanny. Instead, she spent two years training as a homeopath and opened consulting rooms near her home. 'I'm happy having more time for the children, and, if I'm honest, more time for me,' she said. 'I have time to relax and reflect. I have time to spend with the children. Instead of dreading half terms, I look forward to them and plan nice things.'

Lyndsey had the support of her husband when she decided to give up her job. It is hard to risk a change of career without knowing that the bills will be paid. However, that is exactly what Caroline Bird from Chesterfield in Derbyshire did when her children were six and four. She had just divorced and her only real safety net was her parents. If the worst came to the worst and her new career did not work out, she could always move in with them.

From bank clerk to doctor: *Caroline had her first child, Charlotte, when she was 21. Her son Daniel was born two years later. She stayed at home at first, living on her husband's income. Then she returned to her job with a local bank.*

It was when she was 26 that her marriage broke up and Caroline decided to change direction altogether. She and her husband sold their house in Chesterfield and she enrolled as a medical student at Sheffield University. It has meant living in constant debt, but she thinks it has all been worth it.

'We live in two rooms in a shared house in Meadowhead, which is the student quarter of Sheffield,' she said. 'I wanted to get a mortgage on a three-bedroomed house but my credit rating is practically zero. My parents are my guarantors. They've been very supportive.

'The children don't seem to worry about where we're living. We don't go out much because I can't afford to spend much. They go to a good school in one of the best residential areas and they see a lot of my parents, so they feel pretty secure. It costs me about a thousand pounds a year to pay for babysitting and after-school club. I have a little car, which I need when I'm on a placement with another hospital. I will owe about £17,000 by the time I finish my medical degree, about £11,000 on the student loan and around £5,000 on my professional loan. I will also be about £2,000 overdrawn.

*'As far as I am concerned it has all been worth it. I want to become a
doctor and I shall be able to pay back my debts eventually. Sometimes it
has been hard trying to get back every day to see the children, especially
when I was on a placement in Barnsley. I had to telephone the school and
tell them I was going to be late. They were very understanding. I can't
afford after-school club every day. I pick them up at three o'clock two or
three days a week so that I don't have to pay the £10.'*

This is an extreme case. Few mothers would get into such debt when
they had young children to bring up. Yet Caroline's son and daughter
appear to be very happy with their mother's decision and are thriving
at school. They are unaware that their mother is relatively poor. They
can visit their grandparents' house at weekends and play in their
garden. However, Charlotte will be approaching her teenage years
when her mother qualifies. A junior doctor's pay is not very great.
Charlotte may resent the fact that she does not have as much money
to spend as her school friends.

Starting your own business

It may be possible to turn a hobby like cooking into a very profitable
new job. All it needs is a little flair and a lot of determination.

From personal assistant to caterer: *Polly was personal assistant to the
managing director of a public relations company when she moved to Devon
with her husband Pete and their two children, Anna and Sam. She was
already pregnant with her third child. They bought a smallholding in
south Devon. It was a half-hour drive to Plymouth where Pete worked for
the local television station.*

*'We did not have much money after buying the house and the land, and
I thought I might as well make the most of what we had got,' said Polly. 'I
decided to make food for all the local pubs – patés and quiches and pickles.
I got a good response straight away. It earned enough to keep us going and
I could pick my own hours. I would cook in the evenings and take my stuff
round the pubs after I took Anna and Sam to school. I soon had quite a
number of pubs taking my stuff and I would be back to take the kids home.'*

In earlier chapters, mothers who turned their childcare skills into a
business by becoming childminders may have seemed to be changing

jobs. Most, however, are simply tiding themselves over until their children start school. They then return to full-time work. According to Lynn McCarthy, childcare co-ordinator for Leeds City Council, very few are career childminders. She would like to see more become so. The government is like-minded and career opportunities in childminding may become a genuine option.

Casualised work

Mothers often change jobs to gain flexibility in working hours. Bridget was a civil servant in North London. She did general office and reception work and decided to join an office work agency so that she could have more time with her children who were aged 11 and 13.

'It meant I could work when I liked,' she said. 'My husband was earning and the children were both at secondary school. I worked three days most weeks, but I could arrange to take a day off whenever I chose. It meant that half-term holidays were not a problem. I just told the agency I would not be available.'

Teachers, nurses and other professionals with an identifiable skill have always been able to switch to agency work when they have children. However, it is important to be clear about the hours you are prepared to work. Your income is likely to be half your full-time salary if you wish to pick up your children from school every day.

Many other jobs are casualising their workforce. In the past, only a few occupations such as journalism allowed freelance workers. Now the trend is spreading to some of the most established professions such as accountancy. There are many small businesses who do not want to take on a large firm of accountants or have a staff accountant but feel very comfortable with a freelance accountant who will do their books for one morning a week. Freelances no longer seem odd, nor are they looked on as second-best. If you have established a reputation as a full-time worker, a company and its clients is likely to value you just as highly when you go part time.

More part-time posts are being created where none existed before. Some high-street banks, for example, have recently begun to offer lunchtime jobs to counter staff from twelve until two-thirty to cope with the midday rush. It is worth asking friends in your own company what part-time posts they have seen in operation so that you can look out for a vacancy.

Applying for a new job

If you are applying for any kind of new job, you must treat it with the same seriousness as you did when you applied for your present job. Employers want energy and commitment even though they may not be offering full-time work. Many employers like to see candidates putting in effort with their appearance when they appear for interview. The last impression you can afford to give is that you are doing your employer a favour because you are qualified to do other, possibly better-paid, work.

You have to reinvent yourself to fit the new circumstances. The curriculum vitae that you had for your last job application is almost certain to be inappropriate. If you are going for a job in a call centre, your new employer may not be particularly interested in your degree or your professional qualifications. In fact, it may put the company off.

Call centre worker required: *'I had worked for a design company,' said Julie, from Essex. 'The job I was going for was in a call centre which had the kind of hours I needed and was in the right place, near my home. My design qualifications were not relevant. They were much more interested in whether or not I had computer inputting skills and when I could make myself available.'*

Julie had been forced to rethink her career when her two children Charlie and Madeline were born. The cost of commuting to London coupled with her relatively low income had forced her to look for work nearer home. She spotted an advertisement for a new call centre. She rang the number and was interviewed on the telephone.

'It was a little unnerving to start answering questions straight away,' she said. 'They wanted to know what relevant experience I had, whether I had a good telephone manner and what kind of hours I wanted to work. I was invited to take tests and have a face-to-face interview.'

Julie re-wrote her CV to emphasise her previous work with computers, her continuous work record, her strong points. She left out half of her achievements because they were not relevant. She underwent tests and got the job.

'It was the job I needed,' she said. 'I wanted something I could do in the evenings when my husband came home from work. I work four nights starting at six and finishing at eleven. I had a problem with the training because they held that during the day and I had to use a friend's Brazilian au pair to look after the children.'

The other call centre workers are mostly students or mothers with small children like herself. They help each other out. Now Julie has become a supervisor. What seemed like a stop-gap job is turning into a career. There are three or four call centres for financial institutions and utilities that are all close to her home in Essex.

'I am in a good industry. I have been computer-trained and have a good pension scheme and I get sickness pay if I am ill. It is a proper job with a future.'

Many of the same techniques Julie used apply if you decide to change jobs within your present company. You must, to some extent, re-invent yourself to fit the new role. You must try as hard as a newcomer to appear willing and eager. If there is an interview, you must prepare your CV and present yourself as if you were starting from scratch. You are not offering the services of the old you, but the new version.

You are likely to be treated with some suspicion by your new department because you may be known in your old role. If your new job has lower status, it is a mistake to trade on your past glories. It will almost certainly annoy your colleagues. They are not interested in what you did in the past, but in what you do now and in the future. It is far better to behave as if you had never worked for your organisation before. If people are curious, they will ask.

17: STARTING OVER

It is one thing to switch jobs, quite another to start work again after a break of several years. You have to explain your absence. You have to establish your credentials in much the same way as when you applied for your first job many years ago.

This is far easier for mothers than for the long-term unemployed. The changing marketplace means that employers are more ready to accept people who have been out of paid employment for some years, if they can show good credentials from their career before they took a break.

Careers are no longer for life. We are no longer expected to start them straight after school or university and continue them unbroken for forty years. Long-service awards are now as rare as First World War veterans. It is normal for those in their twenties to take years out to travel and discover their strengths.

The rise of the internet has thrown the notion of continuous careers even deeper into turmoil. Businesses are being founded by people with no previous experience in a particular field. They may be young, middle-aged or even elderly. A good idea is a good idea. Your contribution to the success of an internet enterprise rests more on your energy, commitment and deliverable skills than your history of past achievement.

In this context, a mother wanting to start work again after a break to raise a family is no big deal. There is an army of temporary employees standing in for permanent staff in many companies. They are built into the budget. Many are highly skilled with the potential to become full-time staff as soon as the need arises. In my own business, newspapers, temporary work is becoming a recognised route into a journalistic career. A 'temp' may be working as a secretary, but can also offer ideas and articles. Temporary staff are often training for something better and target the kinds of business they would like to work in permanently. A mother who has taken several years out is in exactly the same position.

If you have professional qualifications or you are a member of a trade association or professional body, there will be a recognised route for you to retrain. There will be refresher courses, professional magazines and agencies that can help you get back up to scratch.

There are desperate shortages of teachers, nurses and social workers, especially in the big cities. Anyone working in London knows that there are not enough skilled secretaries to go round.

If you are thinking of going back to your old line of work, it is worth contacting friends who are still in the industry. Some may remember how good you were and help you get back into work quickly. Realistically, however, this is unlikely to happen straight away. You should look on each friend you contact as providing a new thread in your network. Little by little you will be able to piece together which firms are expanding and which are likely to be hiring soon.

Your local Job Centre should be able to tell you of training courses available. These can help you to make the change from domestic work to paid work. They are, however, very time-consuming if you need an income immediately, and they put you on the same footing as all the other newly-qualified hopefuls looking for work.

The most effective way to find a job is to use every network that you have. Parents at the school gates and at school events may be in the same line of business you used to work in. If they know you as the reliable woman who always organises the school fair then that will speak volumes for you if you ask for their help in getting a job. This approach to semi-strangers does not have to be the heart-in-mouth encounter you fear. You can mention casually that you are planning to go back to work in September or October when your daughter or son is settled in at his or her new school and that you are open to suggestions.

You can scour the local papers and trade press for advertisements. If you stopped taking the professional magazines, re-order them. You need to know what is going on. If nothing else, it will help you at your interviews.

These days all experience counts on your curriculum vitae, not just the details which are relevant to your previous career. If you have done your husband's VAT return or tax return or helped out at the play group, these can be put into the gap between finishing your last job and now. So should any refresher courses that you have taken.

Do not apologise for having been out of the workplace. The attitude you should adopt is that you are back now and eager to show that you are as good as you ever were. You must think what strengths you have – unflappability, persistence, good grammar, excellent spelling (old-fashioned virtues that are at a premium nowadays), a clean driving licence, good organisational skills – everything counts.

When you apply for a job, make sure that you detail your strengths. As you are not working, you can offer the company the chance to try you out. This gives you an advantage over someone in a job. The employer can find out if you are as good as you say you are. Those with existing jobs have to give in their notice, usually a month or more. Even if the new employer hires them on a probationary basis, there is as much administration as for an employee who has been headhunted. Wages need to be paid, tax forms filled in. If you can offer to come in immediately on a week's trial you may hit lucky and fill a gap.

As an employer, I can honestly say that these two factors – the willingness to work on a trial basis and enthusiasm – often outweigh any doubts I might have about why a person has not been working. The risk that I am taking in trying out someone who is hungry for a job and determined to show that they can do it is really very little. Never undersell your enthusiasm for getting back to work.

When you apply for any job, you need to show clearly that you have worked out who will look after your children in the holidays – unless the job is term-time only – or if one of them is ill.

I once took on a secretary because her name had been passed on by one friend to another. She had been recommended by her former colleague whose husband was a best friend of a colleague of mine. She had been out of the work place for four years and was returning to work after being divorced. At the interview she explained that she had a childminder for the school runs and that her mother lived not too far away and would look after her daughter if she were ill. She seemed enthusiastic and well-organised.

The recommendations worked well, far better than most conventional recruitment techniques. In the two years she worked for me, she was totally reliable. She has now worked for my successor for three years and is very much valued.

Many mothers prefer a sidelong approach to getting back into work. Rather than applying for a job with full responsibility, you can take a job which will act as a stepping stone to your old career. If you worked on the financial side of a big company, offer to do some similar work for local traders on a part-time basis. Your skills will be more noticeable. Even a job in a local call centre is proof that you are back in the workplace, that you can manage your childcare and get to work on time.

Above all, when you go for your first interview, remember that personality counts far more than absolute qualifications for most jobs. The interviewer is wondering whether you will fit in with the rest of the team. If you can convince a boss of that, you are well on your way.

18: FAMILY FRIENDLY FUTURE

I have seen the future and it works – for both families and employers. Unfortunately, in Britain, it is still some way off. Until companies – even small firms – can be persuaded that family-friendly policies make economic as well as human sense, the promised land will not have arrived. Until we have enough childcare places which are affordable, accessible and flexible, many families will continue to suffer.

A government survey carried out in 1996 showed how much ground there is to make up. Only one in ten employers provided any practical help with childcare. Most were private sector organisations with large numbers of young women workers. Even fewer – five per cent – offered family-friendly policies such as flexible working hours, voluntary maternity benefits, paternity leave or childcare arrangements.

The main reason why mothers do not return to work is lack of adequate childcare, especially good workplace nurseries. There are only 600 in Britain, even though there are big tax advantages to companies who offer their workers such facilities. There are also very few employers who offer vouchers to pay for childminders, nannies or nurseries. Only 3 per cent of employers run holiday playschemes and only one in a hundred helps its workers to find a childminder.

A new era

However, times are changing for the better. A new era in Britain's approach to childcare began with the election of the Labour government in 1997, with an unprecedented 101 women MPs, many of whom had families of their own. The 'gentlemen's club' atmosphere of the House of Commons could no longer be sustained. Family-friendly policies were devised which accepted the reality of family life in which four in ten marriages ends in divorce and many mothers have to do their best alone. A vision of a future in which all parents have access to childcare, in which fathers as well as mothers are encouraged to work part-time to help look after their children, is emerging.

The main short-term task, according to the minister responsible for childcare, Margaret Hodge, is to increase the number and quality of affordable childcare places. Standards by comparison with other European countries such as France have been low. All French mothers have free nursery provision for children aged two upwards. There is a lot of catching up to do. Ms Hodge says in the first two years of the present government, more childcare places were created than in the previous 18 years. In the year to April 2000 the target of 82,000 new places being created was exceeded. There were more after-school clubs and holiday schemes for school-age children. The government says it should achieve its target of one million childcare places in 2001. A vast improvement, but still not enough.

More childminders needed

Childminders are in huge demand but their numbers until recently have been falling, partly because childminding has not been regarded as a serious profession. Many childminders are mothers who have given up full-time jobs to have their own children and want to work from home. Many do not plan to continue as childminders when their own children start school. Instead, they look for better-paid jobs which are often full time. Eighteen per cent leave each year and fewer new childminders take their place.

'There are some very professional childminders who go on to take their NVQs in childcare,' says Lynn McCarthy, a childcare co-ordinator for Leeds City Council. 'But there are others who regard it as a bit of babysitting on the side which will give them a bit of pin money. They go into it with no more of a view than that.'

Better training

Leeds is one of the few cities that insists on all childminders being trained. Even so, the training lasts only eight hours spread over four weeks. 'It's been a patchwork quilt in Britain,' says Ms McCarthy. 'Some local authorities train, some don't. Each had to write its own guidelines and its own rulebook when the Children Act came in in 1991. The Act was very weak. There are three 'musts' and all the rest of the laws are 'shoulds'. A local authority could not go very far in what it put in its guidelines because they could be challenged in court, so they all erred towards the very lenient side.'

This feeble and inconsistent approach to the regulation and training of childminders must change. There must be a national standard and a career path which leads towards many childminders becoming accredited providers of educational places for three- to four-year-olds. The Government has already made the first move by bringing the inspection of childminders under OFSTED, the office for standards in education. Training and Enterprise Councils, the network of regional training centres working in partnership with local authorities and businesses, are also spending money to support childcare training.

'We have got to attract, train and retain childminders,' says Margaret Hodge. 'Currently 70 per cent of childminders have no relevant qualification. We are spending £100 million a year on training childcare workers. Investing in the workforce is key to my agenda.'

More male childcarers

Currently, 97 per cent of people who work in childcare are women. Many are mothers. The challenge for the Government will be to attract men to childcare, too. At the moment, parents are wary of men who apply to look after their children because they fear some may be secret paedophiles. Without proper registers and police checks, this fear will not go away. The government has announced that it will for the first time carry out systematic checks on people working with children aged eight and over.

Quite apart from regulation, men are reluctant to become childcarers. Even primary schools have fewer male teachers. There will have to be a change of culture before this alters. The childcare minister is unusual because she once employed a male nanny. She wants childcare to become a job of choice by far more men and women so that mothers have options denied to them now. 'We have got to give women the choice,' says Ms Hodge. 'We are not forcing them back to work. However, they should not be stopped from going back to work by lack of childcare facilities.'

More nurseries

The number of nursery places in Britain still lags behind many other European countries, though there has been a sudden growth in their number in the last three years. Public provision excludes most middle-income families because access is restricted to those in greatest social need. There is no such stigma in France where families across the income brackets share community nursery facilities run by well-trained staff.

Regulation of nurseries in Britain is also poor. As you may have read in Chapter 3, there are still huge legal loopholes which allow even convicted paedophiles to infiltrate some nurseries because local authorities cannot insist on a police check if a nursery's management does not request it. In the North East of England, nursery staff took pornographic photographs of children in their care. The staff were badly-managed and their criminal behaviour went unchecked.

Once again, the future is a little brighter. All nurseries will in future, like childminders, be inspected independently, under the control of the newly formed Early Years Directorate. This body, under the control of OFSTED, will control all childcare provision outside the home. National standards will be established.

'There are already free nursery places for all four-year-olds,' says Margaret Hodge, the minister for childcare. 'The number for three-year-olds will be doubled during the life of this government, with some 80 per cent of the places coming from the private and voluntary sector.'

Family-unfriendly employers

The biggest battle ahead is to make companies 'family friendly.' We are still in the Dark Ages when it comes to recognising that employees have lives outside their jobs. Even though working mothers are now vital to the success of nearly every enterprise, too many companies continue to act as if they employ only single people with no family ties.

Paid too much to be with her family: The case of JP Morgan, the investment bank, is typical. A recent industrial tribunal decided the firm had not discriminated against a mother who said she had to work fourteen-hour days in the office shortly after her first baby was born. She told the tribunal that she wanted to work an ordinary nine-to-five day and take work home to complete in the evenings but she was refused. The tribunal said:

'Where an individual is... highly paid... the respondent (JP Morgan) had the right to make certain demands in respect of hours and place of work.'

This is outrageous, even if it is a technically sound interpretation of present law. The mother in question, Aisling Sykes, won her case that she was unfairly dismissed for spending too much time with her children. However she lost her claim that her 14-hour working days amounted to sex discrimination.

Her male colleagues may also work 14-hour days and never ask to go home to see their children, but they are fools to do so. The company, which employs 3,500 staff in central London, a third of them women, is wrong if it does not actively discourage them in their folly.

'This is part of the long-hours culture that the City is trying to perpetuate,' said Mrs Sykes. 'There is still the view that you need to be seen at your desk to be a proper worker. No amount of nannies will compensate a mother's need to spend at least a few minutes out of a 14-hour working day with her children, whatever the salary.'

In the long term, if City firms like JP Morgan perpetuate a long-hours culture, it will limit their ability to recruit the most able staff. Even employees without children may soon prefer companies which allow them to have lives outside of work. Who knows, in the future, firms which reward 'short hours culture' may have the competitive edge because they will attract high-flyers who can do their jobs during a normal working day and have time off to do their own thing – hang-gliding, scuba diving, playing in a band, travelling – or even raising a family.

Many companies and organisations in Britain regard families as almost irrelevant to their businesses. They argue that they are in business to provide a service or make a product and that their employees' home lives are their own affair. If you work long hours, it shows your commitment to the company. If a mother or father (or any other worker) cannot accept the terms and conditions of the job on offer, they can look elsewhere. To make concessions would affect profits.

The major task for government is to change this all-or-nothing culture, to persuade all companies and organisations that an 'ethical' approach to parents and other carers is literally good for business. They must be convinced that family-friendly policies make their companies more efficient or even more profitable. If there is money at stake, they will sit up and take notice.

At the time this book went to press, there were moves to introduce paid paternity leave for new fathers. The British government is making moves towards paying a paternity leave tax credit. A ministerial review team was deciding on the level of weekly payments and their duration. This will take some time to come into force. Yet it will begin to transform the attitudes of some employers who consider childcare as having nothing to do with fatherhood. Money will no longer be such a big excuse.

The flexible alternative

Companies like Littlewoods are showing the way forward. It won the 'Employer of the Year' award in 1998/9 for its ground-breaking flexible working practices. It is convinced that family-friendly policies pay. It saves a fortune on recruitment and training. To replace a junior manager earning £15,000 costs around £7,000. At Littlewoods, almost all mothers, at all levels of seniority, choose to return to work. The firm does not have as much absenteeism as the average firm. Its productivity is greatly improved. It also gives it a cutting edge in those parts of its business which need 24-hour operations.

That is not to say that Littlewoods does not have difficulties. Some parts of its business, notably its delivery service, Business Express, have very male cultures. 'Its drivers have a particularly old-fashioned attitude to how they structure their hours,' says Melanie Theobald of Littlewoods' Equal Opportunities division. 'The problem is that they've never thought of doing it another way and nobody has challenged them. We see our job as going to them and saying if you did this it would bring you a benefit.'

BP Amoco is another big firm which has embraced flexible working, at least in its offices. Its oil rigs, predominantly male and by their nature isolated from families, are much more difficult to adapt to new ways of thinking.

The company with its own parents' network: '*People used to pretend they didn't have a family,' says Marion Hansen the maternity adviser at BP Amoco. 'We are changing the culture so that everyone accepts that people want to see their children. Those who don't are rarer . Not everyone uses the opportunities we offer to help them fit in their family life, but it has now embedded itself over the years. Attitudes have changed.'*

BP Amoco has started a parental advisory and networking service which creates an atmosphere where the sharing of childcare between men and women is almost the norm, especially for dual-career couples. The changes have not been without hitches, however. Some men, in particular, are still wedded to the idea of working long hours.

'We have regular workshops for employees about how to balance home and work,' says Marion 'We had a couple recently where the man had a real problem about picking up the children from the nursery. He works all hours in the information technology department. Apparently a lot of the people there stay late because they're concerned that they might be missing out on things. He is still there at ten o'clock at night sometimes. We asked him why he needed to work so late and it was because everyone else did. We explained that he did not have to.'

BP Amoco has three subsidised nurseries, a holiday playscheme, help in planning childcare, a nanny register so that mothers can network with other employees in the firm and share back-up arrangements or even share nannies. It keeps mothers on maternity leave in touch with their colleagues, sends them newsletters and e-mails, invites them in to attend workshops on returning to work, or meetings about developments which will affect their jobs.

According to Marion Hansen, this is not do-gooding. It benefits BP Amoco's business. 'We looked back over the years and we had a return rate of about 60 per cent. Now our return rate is 98 per cent. It used to be the pattern that people worked nine to five, Monday to Friday. Now you do not expect to see people sitting at their desks all the time. About a quarter return to work on a flexible basis which wasn't heard of before. We never get into the cost savings. We like to think of it in terms of our workforce being happy and we keep the skilled staff that we need.'

The savings achieved by family-friendly policies can be quantified. Lloyds TSB recently researched the cost of replacing a counter clerk. It came to £10,000 once everything was added in – advertising for new staff, the time taken to interview candidates, training and the hours lost in supervision of a new employee.

Small businesses

Small businesses have to be equally convinced that such benefits would come to them and that flexible working would not involve a great deal more time-consuming administration. Evidence shows that most flexible workers establish a set pattern of work each week and stick to it, so that, once in place, adminstrative costs are no higher than for other workers. Offering jobs with flexible options also makes it easier for small businesses to recruit and retain staff for hard-to-fill vacancies.

Small is beautiful and flexible: Market Monitor in Buckinghamshire designed its entire schedules around flexible working. It produces business directories, has 26 employees, 18 of whom work only during their children's school terms. It employs university students to fill in for the holiday periods. SEI Micro, a semi-conductor distribution company also based in Buckinghamshire, concentrated its development work on school term-times. Both have saved money on recruitment and training.

Some small businesses are even bartering. One firm of accountants, for example, recently offered to do a nursery's books for one morning a week in exchange for nursery care for its employees at reduced rates. Businesses are giving schools craft materials in return for discount places in their after-school clubs. Some firms with hard-to-fill vacancies are offering school-hours working to attract talented mothers who cannot afford childcare.

Incentives to improve

The government must give incentives for businesses to change their work cultures away from inflexible practices. Childcare initiatives have so far been unimpressive. Childcare vouchers, creches and other assistance have not caught on. The Department for Employment and Education is currently reviewing the options available to employers.

'They will always ask for tax incentives for providing any help with childcare,' says the childcare minister, Margaret Hodge. 'They do not, as a rule, invest in childcare. They do not see the benefits that they get. That is too scattergun and too expensive. It doesn't either increase the supply or subsidise those parents who need it most. They benefit the very well-paid and cannot be targeted. What we need is a culture change. Employers have got to provide some resources and recognise the sound business benefits of retaining staff.'

Audit of business benefits

To that end, the government is working with a business-led alliance to demonstrate the benefits of family-friendly policies to the employer. Led by Peter Ellwood, chief executive of Lloyds TSB, the alliance has leaders from all sectors of industry including some small companies as well as national names. The government is also supporting the charity Parents at Work in its Lloyds/TSB Employer of the Year award scheme for companies and organisations promoting flexible working practices.

The alliance will provide statistics and evidence on the benefits to companies of retaining staff. Companies will be kitemarked for their family-friendly polices and a best boss competition should encourage a few employers to focus on the benefits.

According to Government research, one company with a salary bill of £755,000 saved itself £60,000 in recruitment, retraining and temporary staff costs by being flexible. Six employees who shared jobs were able to take unpaid leave during the school holidays.

Another company with a wage bill of £277,200 was able to save itself £44,200 by family-friendly employment policies. Huber and Suhner UK, a computer parts company, provided shifts in school hours during term time to enable it to attract sufficient staff.

Part-time work encouraged

Part-time working in all its guises is the key to the new culture. There has been a huge growth in this pattern of employment. In 1994, there were around 5.4 million part-time employees, a quarter of the entire workforce. The numbers have grown since with workers concentrated in retailing, banking, insurance and financial services and in the hotel and catering industry. About 86 per cent are women, and the majority have young children.

But with dual-income families becoming the new norm, the number of men who want to work part-time is growing greatly, too. In companies where the change to family-friendly culture is complete, such as BP Amoco in the south-east of England, it is now routine for men to ask for part-time working.

There is a bundle of new laws, both national and European, to protect part-time workers from discrimination. This gives a framework of rights to employees, which are backed up by the threat of tribunals. However, the Government knows that the stick is far less effective than the carrot. It has decided therefore to spread the benefits beyond those most obviously in need.

Carrots not sticks

The Working Family Tax Credit, which began in October 1999, is far more generous than anything that preceded it. Families with income up to £32,000 can get some help depending on what their outgoings are. A parent with a salary of £20,000 and childcare costs of £100 a week will typically get £60 towards those costs each week.

The Childcare Tax Credit for lone parents was introduced at the same time to help pay for the cost of a childminder, nursery or out-of-hours clubs on school premises. It excluded nannies. However, nannies looking after disabled children in their own homes will also be included in new legislation before Parliament. New laws to prevent discrimination against disabled children are also being drafted. Currently, schools can turn away a child with a disability from an after-school club.

Against this background of legal sticks and financial carrots, the childcare minister Margaret Hodge is convinced that something else – peer pressure – will be the main catalyst for changing the anti-family practices of many British firms. If one company can recruit and retain a better standard of employee by offering flexible working practices then its rivals will be forced to copy. If a company can work round the clock and keep its staff loyal and productive by offering shifts which dovetail with childcare, competitors will have to follow suit.

Better regulation

The present mish-mash of regulations will be standardised. The Government has already announced that one body, the Early Years Directorate, will oversee the inspection of all childcare outside the home ensuring national standards. This will go some way towards increasing parents' confidence in the childcare industry. However, the measures do not go far enough.

There are no plans, for example, to extend inspection or any form of registration to nannies. Margaret Hodge says that this is because it would be impossible to keep records of all the people who work as nannies. Some are trained, but the majority are not, and generally they are young and move around the country. They also arrive from other countries.

'If we tried to keep a register it would give a false sense of security to parents,' says Margaret Hodge 'It is also very difficult to establish whether a nanny is bad or has just fallen out with the parents. In many cases it would be the word of the nanny against the parent. It is possible for a girl to work well with one family and not to get on with the next one.'

Nanny register

However, the Professional Association of Nursery Nurses wants all nannies to be registered. They claim some employers are sacking nannies before they reach the age of 21 so they do not have to pay the minimum wage.

I have no knowledge of such abuses of the system. However, I have met unscrupulous parents who are prepared to employ illegal immigrants if it means they get cheaper childcare and avoid paying tax. Their illegal nanny can hardly refuse requests to work unsocial hours. Making it illegal to employ an unregistered nanny (if a register were introduced) might not deter such parents. If it saves them money, they will argue, why not break two laws instead of one? Who is to report them? Their illegal nanny will not, if she wants to keep her job.

The government has decided to set down tougher statutory regulations for nanny agencies. This is a small advance. They will be required to check out the background of nannies. But the Government says it is still important for parents to make their own checks. The Department for Education and Employment has published a booklet – *Need a Nanny?* – which advises them to ask for two proofs of a nanny's identity such as a passport and a driving licence, at least two references from previous jobs, a full employment history and original documents showing qualifications.

This is all sound advice, I am sure, but the only truly effective precaution is the checking out of references. Previous employers usually tell the truth. Why would they lie? If two previous employers say they would really recommend a nanny, you can tell if you trust their word. Getting it firsthand is better than using an agency.

For all the Government's codes of practice, I am not convinced that nanny agencies are to be trusted at all. I shall not forget the agency that slandered the name of an excellent nanny I employed for two years, by quoting a bad reference from her next employer, another parent who believed gossip she had heard from a rival nanny and sacked her without an ounce of proof. If government advice is that you should not rely on an agency's checking system, why bother with the agency and its exorbitant fees at all?

A far better system would be for the government to make it compulsory for nannies to join an approved professional body. The Professional Association of Nursery Nurses might take this role if it complied with whatever conditions the government laid down. We could have state registered nursery nurses. From then on, nannies who were in serious breach of a professional code of conduct would be struck off, but not before any allegations against them had been thoroughly tested in a kind of court. It works for doctors and nurses, why not for nannies and other childcarers too?

Childcare Audit

A one-year investigation into all aspects of childcare and family support was launched in January 2000 by the charity Kids Clubs Network. It is led by Harriet Harman MP, the former Social Services Secretary.

The Childcare Commission, as it is called, was set up to examine how families will structure their work and home life in years to come; what support children and families will need and how current Government initiatives can be built upon to devise the childcare and family support needed for the 21st century. Some 10 to 15 leading industrialists, politicians and specialists will examine the future needs of children and families to propose future developments in childcare.

Harriet Harman said at the launch that one of the main responsibilities of the commssion would be how to make childcare safer and affordable for everyone. 'We will look at who pays for childcare. Should it be employers, parents or the government? Research shows that relatives such as grannies and aunts are playing a much bigger role. Should we be paying for them to look after children?'

Submissions are sought from families and professionals in writing, electronically or verbally. The commission is based at 3 Muirhead Crescent, London E14 9SZ, telephone 020 7512 2112.

Future families

As to the long-term future, the new family will be a thousand different kinds – double income families where dad works part time and mum works full time; families where mother and father live apart; families with nannies round the clock; families with not enough income to afford even a childminder for a few hours; families where mother and father work opposite shifts; families which travel 70 miles a day to leave children with relatives; families with grandparents next door who fit their work around looking after their grandchildren.

The days of stereotypes are over. This is not to be regretted. Many men resented the old culture that forced them to become breadwinners, separate from their families. Many women hated the stifling servitude of being confined to the home when they could have been using their talents elsewhere. We are at the start of a new era of co-operation in which parents of both sexes can work out solutions to bringing up their children and making a living at the same time.

As for the employers of the future, only those organisations which offer the broadest range of working options to mothers and fathers will remain in tune with the times. They must be seen to support childcare actively. At present, nine companies in ten fail to do so. This cannot continue. The round-the-clock economy is with us for good. Women will soon become the majority of the workforce. New ways of organising family life are with us now. Only the most flexible will thrive.

INDEX

Life just got a whole lot easier for you

One of Orange's founding principles is simplicity. We believe that all processes and services should be understandable, logical and easy to use, and as a working mum you will need all the practical assistance you can possibly get. From help with shopping and planning trips away, to your own personal assistant, if you are already an Orange customer you will know that the following range of value added services are in place to make your life easier.

Do you need a personal assistant?

Wildfire is an intelligent and voice activated virtual personal assistant. 'She' is organised, always on hand and works solely for you, for 24 hours a day.

Wildfire is truly unique, and her role can be as simple or as involved as you need it to be. While other mobile phones use Voice Dialling to allow you to call people simply by saying a name or number, Wildfire does far more for you. She manages and sorts messages for you and will make a note of the callers name and number so she can call them back if you ask her to. She even lets you know when you have another call coming in if you are listening to a message or talking to her.

She's there, quite simply, to make your life easier.

Fax me

The Orange Answer Fax acts as an Answer phone for faxes. With your own Answer Fax number you are able to receive faxes on your Orange phone and retrieve them on any fax machine.

When a fax is sent to your Answer Fax number, a text message is sent to your phone to notify you. To retrieve the fax all you have to do is call the Orange Answering Service on 123 and follow the recorded instructions. In addition, the Answer Fax service can receive more than one fax simultaneously, so callers will get through first time whenever they use your Answer Fax number.

Work and Play

If your Orange phone is used to make and receive both work and personal calls, a second line will help you manage your calls more effectively. Each line can have a different ring tone, so you can easily identify whether an incoming call is home or work related. You can also set up a different answer phone message for each line.

The future's bright, The future's Orange

Leave me a message
If you are in a meeting, or are unable to answer calls directly, Orange can ensure that you are discreetly notified when a voice message is left for you. By diverting your Orange phone, calls will be answered by an Orange Representative who will take a message and send it to you in the form of a text message. You can also choose to have your calls answered with either a generic or personalised greeting.

Something for everyone
Orange's range of multi media services offer the user a wealth of informational and transactional abilities. Orange currently offers ITN news services, road and rail information, movie and restaurant listings, ski reports, pages from Loot, and access to lastminute.com amongst many others. New services are being added on a weekly basis and these will include banking services that will allow customers to obtain statements, check balances, and instruct payments.

You can also access orange.net, which will allow you to check your account details online or set up a personal diary that will send your Orange phone a text message to remind you about a meeting or a birthday.

Other products and services will soon include:
Shopping Orange are currently working with both high street retailers and specialist suppliers to provide Orange customers with a comprehensive shopping service that will be accessible via a handset or PC. Customers will be able to browse an increasing number of stores and purchase goods and services electronically in a convenient and secure environment.
Travel The Orange travel service not only provides customers with air and rail timetable information, but will eventually offer ticket purchase and hotel reservation directly through the handset.
Videophone The world's first GSM videophone, a ground-breaking new palm-held device, which will offer video and audio communication, e-mail and Internet browsing. A great tool when you want to keep an eye on your family wherever they are.

A large range of Orange products and services are already in place to help provide people with busy lives solutions to their communication problems, whenever, wherever, and however they choose.

For more information about these and the many other Orange products and services please call 0800 80 10 80.

The future's bright, The future's Orange